A BROWN MAN
IN RUSSIA

LESSONS LEARNED ON THE TRANS-SIBERIAN

A BROWN MAN IN RUSSIA

LESSONS LEARNED ON THE TRANS-SIBERIAN

by Vijay Menon

Edited by John Amor and Ksenia Papazova

Interior layout by Max Mendor

© 2018, Vijay Menon

© 2018, Glagoslav Publications

www.glagoslav.com

ISBN: 978-1-91141-475-9

A catalogue record for this book is available from the British Library.

This book is in copyright. No part of this publication may be reproduced, stored in a retrieval system or transmitted in any form or by any means without the prior permission in writing of the publisher, nor be otherwise circulated in any form of binding or cover other than that in which it is published without a similar condition, including this condition, being imposed on the subsequent purchaser.

VIJAY MENON

A BROWN MAN IN RUSSIA

LESSONS LEARNED ON THE TRANS-SIBERIAN

GLAGOSLAV PUBLICATIONS

Contents

CHAPTER 1: WHY SO SERIOUS? 7
LESSON 12
CHAPTER 2: YOU ARE A LOTTERY TICKET 14
LESSON 19
CHAPTER 3: NO LIMITS 22
LESSON 29
CHAPTER 4: YOU MAD? 31
LESSON 35
CHAPTER 5: OPTIMIZING THE GRAB BAG 37
LESSON 41
CHAPTER 6: THE SPIRIT OF THE LAW 44
LESSON 47
CHAPTER 7: WHO DECIDES WHAT IS OFFENSIVE? 50
LESSON 53
CHAPTER 8: HEAD ON A SWIVEL 56
LESSON 62
CHAPTER 9: KEEP IT TRILL 65
LESSON 69
CHAPTER 10: SOLO STAR 72
LESSON 76
CHAPTER 11: DO THE RIGHT THING 79
LESSON 83
CHAPTER 12: LAUGHING AT YOU OR WITH YOU? 87
LESSON 93
CHAPTER 13: TRY > SUCCEED 97
LESSON 100

CHAPTER 14: TO BELONG	102
LESSON	105
CHAPTER 15: EMBRACING CURIOSITY	107
LESSON	112
CHAPTER 16: ON MULTI-DIMENSIONALITY	115
LESSON	120
CHAPTER 17: THINK LIKE A CHILD	123
LESSON	127
CHAPTER 18: PAY IT FORWARD	129
LESSON	133
CHAPTER 19: THE GOLDEN RULE OF TRAVEL	135
LESSON	139
CHAPTER 20: ENTER THE PORTAL	142
LESSON	147
CHAPTER 21: QUESTION, QUESTION, QUESTION	149
LESSON	152
CHAPTER 22: DO YOU	154
LESSON	155
ACKNOWLEDGEMENTS	157
PHOTOS	161

Avi and I (tan jacket) strolling through Moscow on day two of the trip (don't let the blue sky fool you!)

Chapter 1:
Why so serious?

December 13, 2013
London, England → Moscow, Russia

When I was a child, my parents asked me what I wanted for Christmas. It took no time for me to respond — I requested the Nintendo 64 game *Banjo-Kazooie*.

I woke up on Christmas morning with a distinct feeling of anticipation in my gut. I sprinted downstairs at the crack of dawn and fidgeted impatiently by the tree, eagerly waiting for my parents to rouse. After a seemingly interminable wait, they finally emerged.

"Go ahead," my mom offered. "Open it."

The words seemed so sweet at the time. Tearing apart the wrapping paper, I felt a surge of dopamine as I pulled out my prize. Lo and behold, what was in my hands?

A *National Geographic Atlas*.

"Ah," my mom offered with faux remorse. "Looks like Santa was unable to pick up *Banjo-Kazooie* this time around." My face dropped, as my Dad offered a consolatory, "Maybe next year?"

And in that moment, Santa Claus was dead to five-year-old me.

* * *

The bitterness of that event is not lost on me, but time has mostly dissipated the raw wounds of December 25, 1998. In its place, a countervailing emotion began to incubate — namely, one of appreciation.

Because on that day, my parents inculcated upon me an unconditional love for travel that has carried with me throughout my life.

As I grew up, I became fascinated by learning more about the world around me. I read voraciously, becoming enamored with trivia and Geography Bees.[1] I hauled around a tub of global facts supplemented by recent article clippings from *the Economist*, devised spontaneous lists of top-ten vacation destinations à la *Conde Nast*, and proudly announced my ambitions to aspire to future ambassadorship.

All the while, I had never so much as set foot in neighboring Canada.

So though I could rattle off the name of each world capital with relative ease — including all three of South Africa's — I always felt as a child that actually visiting them was somehow out of reach.

As I entered adolescence, however, that misplaced belief slowly melted away. Tinkering on the Internet, I developed a penchant for travel hacking — scraping error fares, spotting the best routes, and snagging the cheapest flight deals. For the first time in my life, the pages on the *Atlas* began to come to life.

And I explored the world — one flight at a time.

It started small at the onset. But the real turning point was a solitary trip to Guatemala the summer after my freshman year of college at Duke University, living with a host family and sponsoring micro-consignment for local entrepreneurs.

Upon my return, I recall for the first time experiencing a sensation distinctly different than anything I had ever encountered before. Rather than refreshed and rejuvenated, I felt strangely unfulfilled and unsettled — like I didn't quite want to be back.

My exploratory itch had become insatiable, and I hungered for more.

Nay.

I demanded it.

* * *

Fast forward to the summer of 2013.

---

[1] Ah yes, the stuff of nerds. Almost three million 4th to 8th graders competed in the 2017 iteration of the annual competition. If you knew that the Kunlun Mountains lay between the Taklimakan Desert and the Tibetan Plateau, you could have been crowned champion yourself.

That June, as I lounged in my grandparents' residence in Calicut, India for a week before starting a new job at Microsoft, an ineluctable idea planted itself inside my head. I couldn't tell you where it came from, or how it first appeared — only that it was there and that I couldn't stop ruminating on it.

Mongolian Christmas.

Fifteen years to the day of my most crushing childhood disappointment, I felt an irrepressible desire to find myself in the country that I had first learned about in my initially unappreciated but now cherished *National Geographic Atlas*. And so an innocent Google search morphed into hours spent on Seat61.com[2], and an incipient idea soon transformed into a burning desire.

Over a quick Skype call, I pitched my plan to the only people I knew would immediately be receptive — my Duke roommate Jeremy and our fellow classmate Avi.

The two made ideal travel partners, albeit for different reasons. Jeremy, a Knoxville-bred man, possessed not only the appearance but also the qualities of a 19th century frontiersman — intrepid and gritty, with a gnarly red beard to match. Avi, on the other hand, retained an unbelievably laid-back nature that belied his fast-paced Jersey roots — so much so that one could be forgiven for wondering whether he could more aptly be described as carefree or careless.

"The Trans-Siberian Railway? Mongolian Christmas? Say no more."

It was unanimous. We were going to take the train across Russia, through the Siberian tundra, and down into the ancestral home of the Khans. And we were going to do it smack in the heart of winter.

I wish I could provide a more cogent explanation for why this notion of a trip through Siberia took hold of my mind — an all-encompassing story that explains this strange desire and wraps it up nicely in a bow-tied package.

But to contrive a reason would be to deceive.

So rather than lie, I borrow the terse, but sufficient words of John Howard Griffin from his 1959 novel *Black Like Me*.

"I decided I would do this."[3]

---

2   The Internet's pre-eminent source on anything and everything train travel related.

3   A key tenet to life – stop seeking external validation!

And just like that, I was on the runway of snowy Domodedovo Airport in Moscow in December 2013.

* * *

As I shuffled out of the terminal towards border control, I fretted the warped lost-in-translation world into which I was entering. I stepped towards a waving customs agent wearing a fine fur hat and grinned sheepishly, hoping desperately to avoid questioning so as to obscure my ignominious ignorance of the Russian language.

As she flipped to page one of my passport, the woman behind the desk began to laugh uproariously.

And so it began. *Already? What have I done?*

Cackling, the lady pointed down at the passport picture and then looked up at my face.

"You?" she asked with a smirk of incredulity sketched upon her visage.

"That's me!" I wanted to yell.

But I remained quiet and smiled as the woman scanned back and forth, trying to reconcile the commonality between the antiquated passport photo and the person standing in front of her.

At this point, a bit of table-setting is in order. My passport picture was taken when I was a sixteen-year-old high school sophomore. At the time, I had flat, combed hair — the metaphorical epitomization of my constricted living circumstances. When I went to college, I grew out my hair — not as a result of any well-formulated plan, but simply on account of not knowing where to find a barbershop and not wishing to spend any money on it. After a few months, I realized for the first time that my hair is naturally curly and that it settles into a miniature afro without any real maintenance.

I dug the look, and so I've kept it — in its various iterations — ever since. But the picture of me in that passport and of me today are sharply in contrast, even to those who know me quite well. So I couldn't help but laugh along as the customs lady put her bewilderment on full display at the counter.

Unable to make a determination for herself, she motioned over for some other border control agents to join. Before I knew it, I was the center of a burgeoning commotion comprising five separate

Russian officials cramped uncomfortably inside a small customs booth.

Those five sets of heads bobbed up and down from the passport to my face, trying to visualize whether I truly was the same person or if I was some sort of impostor — an existential threat. After all, I'll be honest. It doesn't take much typecasting for me to fit the stereotype.[4]

Eventually, though, concern gave way to laughter — and finally acceptance.

The lady in the fur hat nodded in acknowledgement, mercifully motioned for the other officials to exit the crowded booth, and stamped me through the gate.

My time in Russia had begun.

Dobro pozhalovat'!

Welcome!

---

[4] And the Transportation Security Agency in America seems to agree! Lowlights of airport travel for me include having a "Te Quiero Mama" candle brought from Guatemala for my mother smashed in half in Los Angeles because it "look[ed] like a vessel for illegal contraband", having my afro patted down and searched by an agent with a single white glove in front of the rest of my half-aghast, half-entertained college debate team en route to a tournament in New York City, and being questioned alone for twenty minutes in a back room in Orlando en route to Puerto Rico because it seemed "suspicious" that I was travelling alone – never mind that I was actually with three friends who had yet to arrive at the airport.

Lesson

Like any other human being, I am a mixed bag of character traits — some good, many bad. Every day is an opportunity to improve. But if there is one trait that I can single out as the most invaluable component of my life, it has to be the ability to not take myself too seriously.

To laugh at myself.

Whether it be the day that I wore my polo shirt inside out to work, the occasion that I pulled out a plastic fork at a Chinese restaurant, or the time that I confidently stated a three-point revenue solution to my CEO before going on to forget the third entirely, I would not be able to get through life were it not for my liberal application of self-deprecating humor.

Take, for instance, my experience at customs.

I am convinced that my reaction expedited my entry into Russia, if not ensured it. The fact that I laughed along with the customs lady rather than launching into a fiery rant of indignation helped turn a potentially combative situation into a friendly one.

I have faced similar situations in various other forays abroad. For instance, I was once nearly denied entry into Nigeria when I forgot to bring along a required immunizations card. When asked where the form was, I joked that it was flown away by a dengue fever carrying mosquito. The woman at customs laughed, asked for the real explanation — which was simply that I had forgotten to bring it but was indeed immunized — and then let me through.

Moreover, self-deprecation got me into South Africa on an entirely separate occasion where I should legally have been denied. When my passport was filled with too many visas for the agent at border control to allow me in, I joked that she could either stamp on my endorsements page or suffer through a week with me. She chose the former — and to this day, my passport bears a stray stamp from O. R. Tambo International Airport on an entirely random page.

I have observed the benefits of not taking oneself too seriously not only firsthand, but also via observation. Having worked in technology for several years, I have encountered all sorts of leaders — from engineering managers to business VPs.

The best leaders are uniformly those who make you feel empowered to treat them as peers. They go out of their way to make you feel at ease, demonstrate the humility to admit what they don't know, joke with you, inspire you to be yourself, and motivate you to produce your best work. And, invariably, they have a flip mode that they activate only when necessary.

When they are serious, you know it. And you get it done for them.

These leaders are the type to attract and retain the top talent. And the culture they espouse undergirds Silicon Valley — arguably the most laid back and yet most productive workspace in human history.

Conversely, the worst leaders have always been the ones who make the fatal error of taking themselves too seriously.

You know the type.

The ones who avoid asking questions for fear of looking foolish. The ones who need the center chair at the meeting table. The ones who cannot laugh at themselves.

They are the ones who poison the well for all others around them. And ultimately, if they are not dealt with, their cancer metastasizes to the point that an otherwise unassailable company can fail by virtue of outsized leadership ego alone.

When situations come up in life that can be uncomfortable or potentially embarrassing, we are presented with a stark choice. We can be stiff, angry, and irritable in a shambolic display of defending our proverbial manhood. Or we can laugh, embrace the absurdity of the situation, and let it roll off of our shoulders.

Carl Sagan has made a career out of reminding us of our own insignificance[5] — but somehow, someway, some of us will never get the message to stop taking ourselves so damn seriously.

While I may never fully comprehend the Cosmos, I will always take the core lesson of the cosmic perspective to heart.

---

[5] In sharing an iconic photo of Earth as a miniscule speck on the surface of a voluminous galaxy, Sagan once famously posited that "our posturings, our imagined self-importance…are challenged by [the pale blue dot]."

Chapter 2:
You are a lottery ticket

December 13, 2013
Moscow, Russia

It is difficult to come to grips with reality until you are fully immersed in the moment.

Such was the case as I stumbled through Domodedovo Airport, arriving at the unpleasant realization that I simply was not adequately prepared — neither emotionally nor physically — for this trip.

Not for the weather, nor for the culture, nor for the language — let alone for getting to the hostel.

In fairness, this is often my natural state. While so-called experts relentlessly sing the praises of preparedness, I have always prided myself on possessing a certain level of familiarity — comfort, even — with ambiguity.

There are manifold explanations for this, some reasonable and others more questionable.

On the sensible side, one must admit a certain cathartic effect that being plopped into an unfamiliar circumstance and getting away unscathed has on the human psyche. And so I thrived in impromptu speaking and parliamentary debate in high school and college — forums where preparation had no effect on outcomes and where success was exclusively a matter of do or die.

Perhaps more dubiously, another reason that I preferred the unencumbered route of non-preparedness was to shield myself from the disappointment that over-preparedness so often brings. Some of the most crushing defeats of my life have been in circumstances when I felt poised and ready, only to subsequently fall flat. Conversely, the greatest victories have often been the ones I least expect.

And so, I gradually convinced myself that preparation itself was overrated. At best, you succeed and it feels that much better because you didn't envisage it. At worst, you fail — but at least you could honestly say that you expected just as much.

I have a tendency to be this way.

In a family of worrywarts, my mother often chastised me for my ostensible lack of caring. It's not that I enjoyed tormenting her. Rather, I just never saw the point in worrying. As Epictetus opined in *The Art of Living*, the key to a happy life is to ignore events that exist outside of one's control.

The logical flaw, nonetheless, was that these specific circumstances — the set of conditions I found myself facing in this unfriendly, foreign airport — had not been outside of my control. I had read about Russia. I knew that learning the Cyrillic script would be a boon in my travels around the country. And yet I had willingly chosen to blithely ignore this advice.

In my previous backpacking experiences, I had relied upon someone knowing English — generally, the folks under thirty — to bail me out. But in Russia, things seemed slightly different.

Put simply, I had been *lazy*. And no amount of mental sophistry was going to save me now.

Here's what I knew. I needed to get to a hostel called *Gallina's Flat*. I also had a street address written in Cyrillic that, to my untrained eye, may just as well have been inscribed in Egyptian hieroglyphics. And I did not have a cellular or Internet connection. Armed only with these two items, I proceeded out of the airport and attempted to track down Gallina's pad.

Stepping outside of the double doors, I was met with a blast of cold air like I had never felt before. Hailing from California, I faltered in the face of this icy front. At college in North Carolina, I was the one who frolicked outside taking pictures and throwing snowballs during the occasional light dusting, while the pretentious Northeasterners querulously mumbled derisively about "those West Coast kids."

But this — this was a whole different ballgame. One that would unequivocally legitimize my snow induced curiosity, and likely have the New Yorkers galloping about as well.

All I wanted to do now was board a train to the city and submit myself to its glorious indoor warmth.

Alas, I had no conception of how to purchase a ticket or find out which trains went where. After about five minutes of mildly panicked pacing back and forth on the outdoor platform, I noticed a carriage pulling up. Faced with a choice between doodling outside in the cold any longer and hopping onto a random train — potentially to nowhere — I chose the latter.

In my mind, I made some rough estimations. Generally airports are somewhere between thirty to sixty minutes outside of the city, so I should give this train half an hour before I started to scan vociferously for signs of city life. Of course, there was always the possibility that I had hopped on a train headed the opposite direction — outside of the city. But given the alternative of waiting outside in the freezing cold to figure that out, I judged that this coin toss was a worthy gambit indeed.

With each passing face on the train, I made the same stereotypical judgments that others likely foisted upon me. "She looks," for instance, "like a city slicker. I must be on the right train."

To what degree these estimates were guided by blind hope rather than intellect, I couldn't say for certain. At any rate, it was far too much for comfort.

Approximately half an hour into the ride, though, my fears were allayed, if ever so slightly. Signs of town began to come into view.

Comparing my hieroglyphic directions to the signage, it appeared that I had arrived by pure chance at the correct subway station. But while I breathed a figurative sigh of relief upon miraculously clearing the first hurdle of my journey, I hardly realized in the moment that my woes were just beginning.

As I looked to leave the subway, it dawned on me, somewhat tragicomically, that I did not know the Russian word for "exit."

"No matter," I assumed. "I'll just follow the crowd of people to the nearest escalator and depart."

Unfortunately, it wasn't quite so easy. A bit of context is in order.

The Moscow subway system is a modern marvel. It is the deepest underground subway system in the world. Indeed, sitting on the escalator from top to bottom generally takes between three and five minutes — it's that deep. Throw into play an intricate transfer system, multiple train lines, and not even a rudimentary understanding of the Russian language, and you had me — an indescribably lost individual with no means of human communication, let alone Internet or telecommunications access.

Again, I began to resort to heuristics. I looked desperately for a person of color — someone I assumed could likely speak English and help me out. It did not work, if only for the reason that there were no other people of color.

I walked up to station managers and police officers, feebly offering the word "*exit?*" Cold and unhelpful eyes stared back at me.

For an interminable amount of time, I wandered through the station — up a dizzying array of escalators and back down again, following streams of Muscovites who all seemed to be making transit connections rather than heading home. The only solace was in the fact that here, deep underground, I was shielded from the cold.

After over an hour of perambulation, my efforts finally bore some fruit. I emerged, by chance, from the depths of Moscow's subway into the city. Never had I been happier to be greeted by gale force winds and piercing snow. But there was precious little time to rejoice. It was time to conquer stage three — navigating from the underground subway system to *Gallina's Flat*.

This was no quotidian task. I was dealing with cold like I had never experienced. Moreover, I had never walked on frozen pavement before. Every few steps I stumbled, unaware of even the basics, like how to identify and sidestep black ice.

After much duress, I finally reached a location that I believed to be *Gallina's Flat*. But when I entered the dilapidated parking lot, I could not locate appropriate signage, let alone a phone to buzz. I wandered outside again, disenchanted and alone, as the curtain of darkness began to descend upon Moscow.

As I stumbled up and down the street in vain pursuit of the place, I finally slipped and fell hard on my tailbone, letting out a guttural shout of frustration. At this moment, a shopkeeper who had been observing me roaming the street came out of his shop and asked, "Hostel?"

"Yes," I nodded vociferously, warming heavily to my first human contact since the border examination at the airport.

He pointed at a broken-down door with a rusted button. I raced over to push it, and a welcome voice came over the intercom — that of my friend Avi.

"Yo, man! You here?"
Instantly, my worries dissipated and my regrets seeped away. In spite of those initial trials and tribulations, I had arrived.

Lesson

My Dad once joked, paraphrasing Earl Wilson, that "if you think nobody cares about you, try not paying your bills for a month." I believed him, so I've never fully gone through with testing the hypothesis.

But that first day in Russia truly encapsulated a moment when my own insignificance dawned upon me. Nobody in this country cared if I found my way to *Gallina's Flat* or not. And why would they?

You will never truly be able to feel the abject despair of what it is like to be homeless without actually being so. But if you ever wish to grock some semblance of understanding of what your less fortunate peers go through each night, get a one-way ticket to a country that speaks little to no English, leave your phone behind, and exit the airport with a backpack and no destination in mind.

I've often thought about the disconnect between what we stand for outwardly and what we practice in reality. The person that will castigate you for absent-mindedly throwing the recyclable water bottle into the garbage bin is the same person that will blithely walk by a homeless woman begging for a dollar for her child.

Everyone needs to experience the feeling of helplessness to learn the importance of empathy.

I often think about how lucky my life was — to be born in America (chances 1 in 300), in California (chances 1 in 10), as a male (1 in 2), to two parents (1 in 2), in an upper-class income bracket (1 in 10). I started life with, at minimum, a 1 in 120,000 advantage. And it still took the momentary discomfort induced by an unfamiliarity with culture and climate to reflect on and acknowledge my duty to help others.

Peter Thiel opines in *Zero to One* that "you are not a lottery ticket." Margaret Thatcher once famously stated that her rise to fame was exclusively the result of work ethic and nothing else. We've all heard the basic premise before. If you try hard, you will achieve your dreams.

It's a neat motivational tool and a feel-good soundbite. But have you ever noticed how it's only the ones who make it that are preaching the line?

I, for one, happen to disagree with Mr. Thiel and Mrs. Thatcher. In no way is this a denigration of their respective accomplishments. Both achieved remarkable success in their lives, and that was undoubtedly largely a result of incredibly hard work, passion, and determination.

But let's be honest — there are millions of people who work as hard as Mr. Thiel and Mrs. Thatcher. And hundreds of thousands of them are paid a pittance for what they do.

One may counter that success is a function not only of hard work, but of concomitantly intelligent decisions. Mr. Thiel and Mrs. Thatcher combined the two — hence, they deserve to make more than someone who engages in manual labor for a living. And again, I will not disagree — the two likely combined legendary dedication and sheer brilliance to attain exalted status.

But let's play a thought experiment.

Imagine Margaret Thatcher was born in Somalia and Peter Thiel was born in North Korea — rather than in Great Britain and in Germany, respectively. Do we really think that Mrs. Thatcher would rise to Prime Ministership and that Peter Thiel would go on to found PayPal? Not in their wildest dreams.

In fact, you would almost undoubtedly never have heard of either of them.

Thiel and Thatcher are products of many things — old-fashioned hard work, incredible planning, devotion to detail, ingenuity, and attention to craft. But to deny that they are also the products of luck is dishonest.

It is, more pointedly, insidious.

It does a gross disservice to society. And frankly, we should start to reject the motif of hard work alone begetting appropriate desert wherever and whenever we hear it.[6]

---

6   I get it – it feels good to pat ourselves on the back! But why do we somehow believe that acknowledging our own success must necessarily be mutually exclusive from recognizing that there are others who are highly competent and capable, too?

The Walton family — consisting of six members of the family of the founder of Walmart — owns more wealth than the bottom 40 percent of all Americans, denizens of the richest nation state the planet has ever seen. Just eight men — including the likes of Jeff Bezos, Bill Gates, and Carlos Slim — possess more money than half of the world's population.

Think about that for a second.

We could comfortably fit a singular van with more combined wealth than that of the "bottom" 3.5 billion people. Bill Gates and Marc Zuckerberg work hard — but do they work 375 million times as hard as the rest of us?

There is no sane argument that excuses such a gross disparity in income. And when it comes down to it, Gates and Zuckerberg themselves would tell you that their success is largely a product of luck in addition to grind — a fact evidenced not only by media statements, but also by highly public commitments to donate their respective fortunes upon expiration.

When good things happen in life, it is okay — indeed, it is natural — to feel proud. By all means, let's pat ourselves on the back. Success is quite rarely a singular function of chance.

But let's stop to acknowledge our luck as well.

Only then can we begin to feel a real sense of empathy for those who deserve it the most. And perhaps, then, that empathy will compel us to devote our lives to lending a helping hand to those who could use a dose of good fortune in their lives, as well.

Chapter 3:
No limits

December 13, 2013
Moscow, Russia

Gallina, a bespectacled old woman with salt-and-pepper hair and an avuncular aura, greeted me warmly at the door.

"*Privet!*"

Hello.

"Did you have any trouble getting here?" she asked in broken English.

I chuckled.

"If only you knew. . ."

Boy, was I glad to see Gallina. She was a crazy cat lady — just my type. I ran upstairs, barely avoiding a motley assortment of felines, and located Avi who was sprawled out on a plush couch.

"How did you get here?" I inquired. "Those directions were indecipherable."

"It was easy, man. I learned some basic Cyrillic on the plane ride over."

Of course. Avi — always learning.

I wanted to relax after the traumatic ordeal of getting to the place, but Avi was limber and ready to go.

"I've been waiting for you guys forever! Let's get out of here!"

"But shouldn't we wait for Jeremy?"

"He's a grown man, he'll figure it out," Avi retorted.

"Dude, it's really not that easy. We should probably wait just in case," I offered.

"Come on, man!"

I relented.

And so we ventured back out into the tundra to the first place that drew us in — McDonalds. Before you judge, let me explain.

While the brand is associated with disgust in the eyes of most millennials, I have to admit that I've always been somewhat of a McDonalds apologist. It's not because I love their food — though I could always be down for some Chicken McNuggets or a Fillet-o-Fish. Rather, it is because McDonalds has always bailed me out on my various jaunts abroad with the enticement of free Internet.

Whether it be "Wifi Gratis" in Barcelona, "Wifi Gratuit" in Marrakech, or "Free Wifi" in Dublin, I've always made a habit of scoping out the nearest McDonalds whenever I enter a foreign land. It has become a source of comfort — a beacon of support, alluring in the sense of a modern-day Statue of Liberty, except for that the "huddled masses" yearn not for freedom, but for the Internet that their domestic cellular providers so cruelly deprive them of.

So we didn't enter for the food. That, of course, would be silly.

We came to speak with the locals.

I pulled out and dusted off my trusty Microsoft Surface, ventured over to translate.google.com, and typed in the only two questions that needed to be asked that night.

"Where should we eat?" and "where can we get vodka?"

In our informal survey of several bemused Russian Big Mac aficionados, we gleaned two general themes. Vis-a-vis the former question, the response generally entailed an extended index finger pointed towards the counter in front of us.

Made sense. In fact, it would be kind of odd if a local were to suggest a place other than the one they were eating at.

With respect to the latter, a giggle, and then the word "*vezde.*"

Everywhere.

We could get vodka everywhere.

We ventured out into the cold, and sure enough, stumbled right into a local corner store to pick up a fifth. At this location we encountered the first of many incidents of Russian alcoholism, portending what the future had in store for us. We observed two husky men in their mid-fifties stumbling up and down the aisles in pursuit of another bottle, occasionally knocking items off the shelf.

I've often thought that working the late-night shift at a 7/11 convenience store in a large American city may be the worst job in the world. It seems that every other video that makes its way to *WorldStar*[7] involves a 7/11, some seedy character, and the threat of imminent violence. Moreover, my personal experiences at the chain make me recoil at the thought of such a vocation. But given a choice between manning the cash register at a 7/11 and working as an alcohol vendor in Russia, I would scurry to the 7/11 in a heartbeat and express the deepest and utmost gratitude in doing so.

Perhaps I'm being a little overdramatic. These *borrachos*, as so many dipsomaniacs are, were the friendly type. And it was a fitting start — and, perhaps, a precursor — to what the night would become; or rather, what it would devolve into.

We exited the store basking in the dual luxury of not only being able to drink legally (Avi and I were both twenty at the time, under the legal drinking age of twenty-one in America), but also being able to do so audaciously in the streets without the aid of a trusty brown bag. We ventured over to an appealing looking hookah bar to relax and soak in the surreality of it all.

Therein lay one of the great paradoxes of travel — escaping to exotic lands, only to seek refuge in normality.

Hookah in Russia? Paying premium money for an experience at a tony lounge that could have been enjoyed at home while spurning opportunities to do something unique more cheaply? It was a poor choice — and like all similar mistakes in travel, it left us feeling rather dimwitted. Ready to make better decisions, we packed up our things and headed back to *Gallina's Flat*.

We arrived expecting to encounter the grizzly and bearded visage of Jeremy. Yet when we returned to the flat, we did not hear the familiar husky baritone of his voice.

Avi and I were slightly concerned. While we were known for our general aversion to readiness, Jeremy was renowned for his cavalier attitude towards preparedness. Moreover, Jeremy was a man of many bizarre idiosyncrasies.

Due to some strange combination of bashfulness and pride — I've never figured out which — he refused to ever ask for directions. Indeed, Jeremy found the thought of asking for assistance in any circumstance, no matter how narrowly tailored — be it a food recommendation from a waiter at a restaurant, or a navigational

---

7   For those not in the know, think of *WorldStar* as R-Rated *YouTube*.

question to a native in a foreign land — to be not only extraneous, but overtly offensive.

So if indeed Jeremy were lost, there was a good chance that he would be out on his own for a while.

"Should we just head out without him?" Avi asked.

The fact that we considered this possibility lends some insight into the dynamic of our crew. It's not that we were selfish. Rather, we knew each other quite well. The three of us, at heart, are wildly self-reliant — to the point of potential danger.

If one of us were missing for twenty-four hours, it would be no big deal.

Seventy-two hours? Maybe worth inquiring via text, but still not out of the realm of the usual.

A week? Perhaps we might start to take it seriously, but in all likelihood we would chalk it up to a case of youthful adventurousness.

Just as I was about to respond affirmatively, we were greeted by a familiar gravelly rasping.

"HA-HA!"

Jeremy jumped out of a side closet, dressed in his famed airport shirt — a ragged button-down befitting of his rugged Tennessee roots. After a round of dapping and fist bumps, we settled down in the room and began making plans for the night and the trip.

Avi pulled out our recently acquired bottle of vodka, and we passed the bottle around taking pulls "to the face" — in other words, drinking directly from the bottle. What passed as extreme to an American, we would soon realize, was merely quotidian to a Russian.

As we were in the midst of getting sozzled, another traveler checked into the four-bedroom place that we were staying in.

"Hi! What's your name?" I inquired.

Her name was Kim, and she was an Irish educator stationed in Abu Dhabi who had chosen to take a trip out to Siberia. She was looking for a quiet night, but unfortunately, she had picked the wrong venue for that.

"Why don't you come out with us?" Avi implored.

Kim looked skeptical — as would most, given Avi's oft haggard appearance. But Jeremy knew the key to an Irishwoman's heart was alcohol, and he handed her the bottle.

Once she took her first shot, resistance was futile. The importunate Americans had convinced her to join us on our first night out.

"Alright, let's make moves!" I shouted at the consummation of an hour of pleasantries and light conversation in the flat.

We ambled out and wandered aimlessly through the streets — our typical means of transportation — before entering a dance club called *Crisis*. Much to our chagrin, we found the bar completely packed but the dance floor entirely desolate.

Never ones to be bashful, Avi, Jeremy, and I set out to change that. Kim looked on bemused, hanging out on the upper deck.

It must have been a strange sight to see. This motley squad of three — two swarthy, and one Tennessean — grooving to hard Russian rock on the floor of a club in a traditional Muscovite neighborhood. But our presence had an almost magnetic effect on the dance floor.

Within minutes, the floor was packed and the outskirts were filled with curious Russian bystanders. Various attempts at communication were made, but nearly all of them failed due to the combination of alcohol, music, and language barriers. Despite this, the three of us had a great time — and judging by the flow of the crowd from the bar towards the dance floor, it seemed like the locals enjoyed our presence as well.

After a couple of hours of good dancing and banter, we headed over to a nearby club called *Propaganda*. At this point, I was tired of dancing, so I spent the next hour roaming the concourse and interweaving my way between people — taking in the absurdity of it all.

Here I was in Russia, an ostensible political enemy, with not even a modicum of understanding of the language — and I was having the time of my life. Despite my distinct inability to communicate, I could sense that the people — particularly those under the age of thirty — seemed supremely friendly. They wanted to connect, if only we could find a way to do so.

As the clock approached 3:00 AM, Kim emerged from the shadows looking bereft of color — presumably from jetlag, but perhaps from culture shock and having to keep up with three twenty-year-olds — and pleaded with us to head home. We agreed to oblige, but not without first making a stop at a local *Subway* sandwich shop.

Falling back to the familiar, once more.

While there, Jeremy committed the faux pas of referring to Kim as an "Irisher." For whatever reason, this caused Kim to storm off home by herself in the pouring snow. We were high off life though, so we declined to follow and continued enjoying the food and company.

After we finished, we headed back to Gallina's.

I skipped back and forth through the streets, slipping and sliding in the snow. But as I weaved across the empty, iced-out road, I heard a shout that froze me in my tracks.

"Stop!" shouted a baton-wielding officer, delivering a command that is the same — and equally harrowing — in both Russian and English.

His head was obscured by a balaclava, but I could still feel the anger emanating from beneath the thick cloth. Panicked, I scurried into a dark garage across the street. I heard Avi mumble, "oh boy" while Jeremy's footsteps followed me into the garage.

The officer, of course, was not fooled.

Incensed that his orders had been summarily ignored, he stomped into the garage with an aura of righteous indignation and sternly questioned me in Russian, threateningly waving his baton just inches from my face. Huddled in fear, I failed to form words, my lips quivering soundlessly.

Right before the officer was about to make a move to strike, Jeremy stepped in.

"*Sprichst du Deutsch?*" he asked.

Do you speak German?

Warily, the officer nodded affirmatively.

As Jeremy proceeded to tell me when the incident had died down, he explained to the officer that I was new to town and did not fully understand proper conventions. He promised to personally take it upon himself to prevent me from any future lawlessness — a deal that the officer begrudgingly accepted.

There he was. My white savior[8] coming to the rescue again.

---

8   Half-pejorative, half-affectionate, and 100% sarcastic, "white savior" is a term I frequently bestow upon Jeremy for his uncanny ability to rescue me from unsavory interactions with law enforcement. His presence has exonerated me on many occasions, including the time an officer in Indianapolis pulled me over but chose to let me go because I "associated with good people."

Thankfully for me, Jeremy was a German major at Duke. Due to continental proximity, a nontrivial portion of Russia's population speaks German. Insofar as these forces collided at that precise moment, I was spared a beating — or worse, a night in a Moscow jail cell for the minor offense of "joywalking."

Nonetheless, I resolved not to test the authorities again during my stay in Russia. I walked home in a straight line, tiptoed past the snoring Kim, and went directly to bed.

Night one was in the books. I had survived — just barely.

Lesson

The British sci-fi author Arthur C. Clarke is most renowned for penning the classic *2001: A Space Odyssey*. Personally, though, I am more enamored of a lesser known work of his — 1962's *Profiles of the Future*.

In it, Clarke introduces the first of three famous laws. It reads as follows.

"When a distinguished but elderly scientist states that something is possible, he is almost certainly right. When he states that something is impossible, he is very probably wrong."

Clarke's comment is tailored to the world of science, but I've taken the liberty of cross-applying it to the panoply of life's domains. My interpretation of Clarke's comment reformulates it into something nearly indistinguishable from Kevin Garnett's indelible proclamation upon winning the 2008 NBA Championship over the Los Angeles Lakers.

"Anything is possible!"

Being in Russia was a dream come true. It was the culmination of an inchoate idea turned into an ineluctable reality.

Backpacking wasn't an ambition, let alone a fantasy of mine growing up — but a trip to Guatemala my freshman summer of college turned it into a fiery passion. Shortly thereafter, I would have traversed six continents and more than sixty countries, finding myself everywhere from Bulawayo, Zimbabwe to Ponta Delgada in the Azores.

Upon hearing of my travel itch, friends and family constantly warn of the need to be careful. While their concerns are well-intentioned and appreciated, I'd argue that they are largely misguided.

After all, I am from America — one of the deadliest places on Earth. Indeed, I am far more likely to be the victim of random gun violence in almost any major American downtown than I am to be the victim of any sort of crime in almost any other place — Africa, Asia, Europe, or otherwise.

And yet despite this reality, images of travel still conjure up visions of fear in the eyes of most Americans. This isn't their fault — they haven't seen the world, and the media has conditioned them to believe that the rest of our planet is nothing more than a third-class post-apocalyptic wasteland.

It is, as Nigerian author Chimamanda Adichie says, "the danger of telling a single story."[9] And therefore the burden falls on all of us — and most crucially, on the traveler — not just to challenge the narrative, but to expand upon it. The story of Russia, like the story of America, is multi-faceted and complex.

Nonetheless, many who get past the fear factor of travel — who saunter bravely past the single story — still believe that the exorbitant cost of travel surely blocks them from experiencing the world. And while travel is always a privilege that should not be taken lightly, the reality is that for a growing number of people, this argument is becoming more and more tired by the day.

Between the combination of filtering for the best price, geo-locating to take advantage of currency arbitrage, and even email sign-ups that do the work for you and deliver the top deals to your inbox daily, most desirous of some form of travel can find a package that meets their budget and allows them to get out of the country.

And so my takeaway from night one in Russia is one that I had always felt, but perhaps came through most profoundly in that moment.

You can do anything you want to do. Life has a strange way of setting you up with unexpected encounters.

Seize them, because you only get one life and it's way too short to spend in just one place.

---

9   Yes, she admits, the story of Nigeria does include chapters on poverty and corruption. But it also consists of stories on higher education, camaraderie, and shared bowls of jollof rice. It is just as important that the world hears the latter stories as they do the former.

Chapter 4: You mad?

December 14, 2013
Moscow, Russia

I woke up the following morning with a slight headache, but a concomitantly ineluctable desire to hit the road — or whatever frozen remnants were left of it — and keep exploring. There was one matter that needed to be settled first, though.

We had a train to catch that evening — headed west to St. Petersburg where we would officially kick off our journey across Russia.

In this instance, our group's unsavory propensity to avoid planning reared its ugly head once more. Missing this departure would put our scheduled timeline in serious jeopardy. Logistically, it would render the notion of a Mongolian Christmas all but impossible. Perhaps most crucially, it would threaten the raison d'être for the entire trip — boarding the Trans-Siberian Railway.

We were on a tight schedule, and we needed to lock down that ticket. There were, however, two problems.

First, we had no conception of whether tickets to St. Petersburg were available that specific evening. While we assumed there would be a means of getting from point A to point B, none of us had undertaken the research to verify the assumption. Second, we still didn't speak a lick of Russian — which would make obtaining the tickets problematic in and of itself.

Vis-a-vis the latter consideration, Gallina ended up being our savior. The kindly old lady who owned the flat in which we stayed in Moscow spoke limited English — or, as she would call it, Russian English.

After we explained our situation to her, she composed a letter for us in such impeccable handwriting as to obviate curiosity over who the real authors of the message were. She instructed us to take this document to the train station and show it to the conductor, explaining our need for three third-class seats on an overnight train to St. Petersburg.

As we set off to depart, Jeremy handed the fateful letter to Avi, instructing him to hold onto it while he suited up in long johns and a Patagonia jacket. This seemingly trivial interaction would take on added gravity some thirty minutes later when we emerged from the subway station and headed towards the main train station where we intended to purchase our tickets to St. Petersburg.

"Avi, let me get that letter back," Jeremy intoned, outstretching an upward palm.

Avi began to search his pockets — casually at first, but gradually crescendoing into a frenzied flailing of the arms. It started to become clear that he had misplaced it.

A sheepish look descending upon his face, he shrugged in defeat. The letter, it seemed, was lost.

Normally even-tempered, Jeremy erupted.

"How could you lose a sheet of paper? You held it for one second. How could you not hang onto a piece of paper for *one second!*" Jeremy shouted, putting on a clinic in hyperbole.

"I don't know, man. . ." Avi stammered, taken aback by Jeremy's out-of-character explosion.

But lamentation would not procure our train tickets or bring back the letter. Disheartened, we continued walking towards the train station, hoping that we could get by with limited words and maniacal gesturing — a combination that thus far had taken us to various parts of the globe with a surprising degree of success.

As we entered the station, Jeremy pulled a note from his chest pocket.

"Guys," he offered bashfully, "I guess Avi had actually given the letter back to me. I have the paper."

Avi and I looked at him, the latter in bemusement and the former ready to pounce. Yet for all of his impetuous outbursts of rage, I credit Jeremy with this — he is always gracious in copping to his faults.

Indeed, Jeremy is a man driven by an unrelenting pursuit of fairness.

He is the guy who will pick up someone else's litter, the athlete who will refuse to call a foul on game point, and the counsel who you can generally trust as an arbiter in any dispute. So an ostensibly tempestuous incident that likely would have caused drama in any other group passed quietly here, as Jeremy profusely apologized to Avi and acknowledged the peccadillo of his quick temper.

Shortly thereafter, we pulled up to the double doors of Moscow's main train station. Armed with Gallina's letter, three winning smiles, and a brisk "*Privet!*" we felt prepared to handle the task at hand.

Sadly, we had failed to account for the difficulty in finding the proper vendor to purchase the tickets.

Entering the station, we were faced with two pathways — one leading to a set of doors and counters on the right and another leading to an almost identical set of doors and counters on the left. As both appeared outwardly to be purveyors of tickets, we chose the set on the right at random and proceeded to the first vacant counter.

"*Privet!*" we chimed in chorus, dropping the letter off at the counter.

The man at the desk greeted us with a stern face, briefly skimmed the letter, wordlessly returned it, and pointed across the way to the other side of the hall.

"No problem," I thought. "We just chose the wrong side."

The three of us scuttled to the other end of the hallway and proceeded again to the next vacant counter on the left side. We repeated our ritual of saying hello and dropping off the letter.

This time, the lady at the counter — with an icy demeanor to rival the man across the way — responded in an equal and opposite manner. She, too, extended an index finger, this time back across to the set of doors and counters we had just migrated from.

"Wait, but. . . he told us come here?"

We tried to reason but to no avail. Without a mastery of the language, we lacked options.

Feeling defeated, we trudged back across, waiting for an open counter. To our misfortune, we were again called up to the counter of the original man who had sent us across. We let the group behind us pass and waited for the next opening, hoping for better luck with another provider. After being called up to the desk by a fresh face, we plopped down the letter for a third time.

This was the literal embodiment of Einstein's classic definition of insanity — doing the same thing over and over and expecting different results. For all of his genius, I began to wonder if the physicist could have made it in Russia.

The purveyor again dropped the letter with such alacrity that I almost felt as if she could not possibly have read it, and motioned to the other side. We moaned in unison, and just as Jeremy was picking up our bags to depart, I shouted, "*Nyet!*"

No. I refused to be someone else's problem.

Surprised, the woman cocked her head to the side and looked at me. I picked up the crumpled letter and pushed it back into her hands.

"St. Petersburg," I said.

Slowly, she pulled out a calculator, multiplied a base fare by three, and handed it to me for review. I pulled out my rubles and paid. We had three tickets on the overnight to St. Petersburg.

All it took was a little pressure.

The trip was no longer in jeopardy. It was back on.

Lesson

If you only have three letters in the English language and you desire to inflict maximal emotional damage on those around you, utter the following characters in this order: "D-M-V."

Every American is familiar with the Department of Motor Vehicles. The organization has embedded itself into the psyche of the American fabric as a real-life manifestation of the problems inherent within bloated bureaucracy promulgated by unwanted and unnecessary government intervention.

Seemingly every trip to the DMV is a nightmare of Sisyphean proportions. From the unnecessary paperwork, to the interminable waiting times — from the rudeness of the employees to the logjam to enter the building — you seemingly couldn't script a poorer customer experience.

And yet, as with all things, being upset about it makes the experience no better.

I am reminded of Principal Sweeney's famous words to the white supremacist Derek Vinyard in *American History X*. Vinyard devotes his life to hate after his father, a firefighter, is gunned down by an African-American gang member in Southern California. Sweeney asks, "Has anything you've done made your life better?"

As David Foster Wallace opined in *This is Water,* his keynote to a group of graduating seniors from Kenyon College several years ago, the key to sanity in life is to become truly "well-adjusted." Being well-adjusted means taking a step back every now and then to view yourself as something other than the center of the universe.

In the context of the DMV — or the Russian train station — it means giving the benefit of the doubt to the employee who you feel is being rather shrill with you. This means keeping your mind open to the *possibility* that he may simply be having a bad day, but is not an awful human being at heart.

In the context of Avi losing the sheet of paper, it meant lending credence to the possibility that this may not be representative of a core character flaw, nor an indication of his utter inability to be trusted with any semblance of responsibility — but rather that Avi may just have had crummy luck that time around.

Of course, our initial assumptions may be right. The employee at the Russian train station may be an insolent slacker and Avi may be an incompetent buffoon — and, to be honest, I sometimes err on this side of the fence with respect to my opinion of him.

But it doesn't help us to think these things. And much of the time, we will be pleasantly surprised to find out that we are wrong — as Avi constantly reminds me.

More importantly, we will find that we are happier when we don't fall into the trap of reductionism any time something doesn't go entirely the way we planned it. And we will be less likely to make such generalizations when we become more aware of the need to be well-adjusted — meaning, when we recognize that we are not the only people in the world who matter.

I went to Russia knowing that things may not always go according to script. Indeed, that is part of the thrill that I had bargained for in planning the journey. Being well-adjusted helped me to survive.

If I had lost faith, or reacted angrily to every mis-step, I may never have made it to *Gallina's Flat* in the first place.

Chapter 5:
Optimizing the grab bag

December 14, 2013
Moscow, Russia

Having obtained our tickets, we waltzed out of the train station triumphantly and commenced our sightseeing agenda.

First stop — the Kremlin.

Russia's seat of government carries a nefarious and almost mythical aura in the American psyche. It is the nucleus of all that the Western world despises — a potent symbol of corruption and an embodiment of shambolic governance, the mere sight of which is guaranteed to give any American diplomat neuralgia (well — except, perhaps, Donald Trump).

To born and bred Americans, a visit to the Kremlin is akin to entering the lion's den. We were the enemies at the gates.

Except it didn't feel that way to me.

I was always allergic to the particularly virulent strain of nationalism that runs through America.

Don't get me wrong. I love the USA.

But I subscribe to the notion — laid out eloquently by Dr. Cornel West, among others — that a child's life is just as valuable whether they were born in Nicaragua, Yemen, Saudi Arabia, France, America, or Russia. Politics may divide us, but people are people. At the end of the day, these arbitrary borders cannot and should not divide what uniquely binds us all together — our humanity.

So to me, the Kremlin seemed nothing more than a chintzy consortium of buildings I had viewed on Google Earth a plethora of times prior.

As we approached, however, my skepticism gave way to awe. This is all the more remarkable for the fact that I am far from an easy critic to please. Upon visiting the White House for the first time, my sister and I both stood aghast in stony silence before peppering bystanders with questions.

"Is this really it? Why is it so small?"

I was impressed with the Kremlin from afar. But to enter and get the full experience was a more vexing problem.

One of the most annoying things about Russia was the lack of signed crosswalks. Indeed, the country must rank near the bottom in the world on any objective scale of pedestrian friendliness. But, as tends to be the case in foreign lands, a certain level of anomie kicks in.

"Ignorance is no excuse for the law," is a tougher argument to make when the law itself is written in a language you don't understand. This made it easier to ignore traffic laws and to skid across icy roads dangerously, illegally, but most importantly, efficiently.

And today, that would have to be the mode of operation.

Upon entering the complex, we were dismayed to encounter a series of long, winding lines. To make matters worse, I had decided to leave my underlying thermal T-shirt and North Face Jacket at *Gallina's*, fooled by the clear blue sky into rocking a singular parka.

It was a hard lesson to learn — one that led to a total stultification of the senses and a chilling of the nerves — but needless to say, one that I would fail to repeat for the duration of the trip. As George W. Bush once famously stammered, "if you fool me once, you can't get fooled again!"

When we got to the front of the line, I asked for a student discount pass to enter the facility. The man at the counter perused my ID card and then mumbled in broken English — which at this point was the most welcome language my ears could possibly record — "this is insufficient."

I stared at the card and asked him, "Why?"

"It is not the standard student ID card. Your card must meet these guidelines," he replied, pointing at an inscrutable poster with certification requirements behind her.

At the counters to the left and right of me, I heard the same conversation being replayed with Avi and Jeremy — both of whom had already accepted the verdicts and forked over the cash for their individual general admission tickets.

"Wait a second," I retorted. "I am a student. Look, it clearly shows that I go to university," I said, handing back the card with a smile.

The man behind the glass window shrugged his shoulders nonchalantly, then pulled out a calculator and subtracted the cost from my price.

Score. It was becoming a theme in Russia — always ask twice.

Satisfied, I joined Jeremy and Avi outside the line and quietly reveled in the glory of a broke college kid discount.

Once inside the Kremlin, we encountered a labyrinth of buildings of myriad shapes and sizes — government offices, cathedrals, and so forth. In my mind, there exists an exalted vision of these edifices, resplendent and grandiose in stature against the icy backdrop.

Nonetheless, something makes me think that perhaps a tiny reason for my enthrallment was the fact that these buildings served as a constant refuge against the freezing cold outside. This led us to explore every nook and cranny of a complex that may, on a sunny California day, have passed for merely quotidian architecture.

Nevertheless, we truly enjoyed visiting the various monuments of the Kremlin. Jeremy, in particular, harbored an unhealthy obsession with a giant cannon in the center of the complex. After numerous exhortations, we were finally able to pry him away from the scene — but not before he was able to sneak in dozens of selfies.

After a couple hours wandering through the Kremlin, the three of us sought to escape the bone chilling cold and fill ourselves up with some hearty alimentation. The most expedient option was *Sbarro's*, a kitschy pizza joint that would warm us up and satiate us on the cheap — or so I thought.

Inside the restaurant, I became fully aware of my outsider status. Gaggles of Russian women stared at me, some snapping pictures stealthily on their camera phones and others giggling quietly to themselves.

Yet there was nothing overtly hostile or upsetting about their behavior. I was merely different, eliciting bemusement in the same way that a white camel or a blue lobster would. I could live with that.

Indeed, I would come to enjoy it.

At the counter, I ordered two slices of pizza and a salad. The cashier pointed at the register, and plangently declared, "One thousand five hundred rubles."

"Great," I thought. "Only three dollars. What a steal!"

I swiped my credit card pell-mell across the magnetic stripe, only to realize milliseconds later that my penurious self had just made a devastating error of calculation. Those three dollars were actually thirty. One of the pratfalls of travel is the constant need to do the mental math on transactions in foreign currencies, and I had fallen prey to it once more.

I sighed deeply, collected my food and ate in silence. Pricy food can be forgiven when it's good — but this was inexcusable. Frustrated, I crumpled into my seat and silently fumed.

At this moment, a homeless man peered through the window and gestured towards his mouth. While I try to be charitable to the less fortunate, I must admit that I often fail to fulfill my eleemosynary obligations. This situation was serendipity at its finest. With quickness, I abjured my hatred of *Sbarro's* and rushed out of the door to deliver the food to the grateful vagabond.

On a day of missteps, the meal turned out not to be a complete disaster after all.

Lesson

One of many traits I particularly respected about my grandfather was his otherworldly ability to make the most out of every situation. He was a man who never visibly lost his temper towards me growing up, even when my petulance clearly warranted it.

On the sole occasion that he did raise his voice with me — one that I assuredly bore the brunt of the responsibility for — he repented immediately and stayed up the whole night in remorse.

This is all the more remarkable for the fact that my grandfather's progeny turned out quite dissimilar to him — tetchy, irritable, and easily annoyed.

Little things tend to set us off. Imperfections annoy us. They limit our ability to enjoy ourselves. They distort our pre-conceived notions. And they leave us feeling unfulfilled.

In and of itself, this would seem natural.

Life is, in many ways, robustly unfair. Each one of us has different circumstances, entirely outside of our control, that either impair or preclude our ability to succeed. This directly contradicts the notion that we earn what we deserve.

Such a mantra necessitates that we all start on common ground and that we all get a fair shake. But the truth is, we all are born onto different rungs of the proverbial ladder. It is in the interests of the rich and powerful to obfuscate this reality from us because it makes us feel that our ostensible failure lies entirely in our own hands and that their seeming success is entirely the result of magnificent desert.

Such a narrative is pernicious, indeed. Nonetheless, its obvious falsehood manifests itself in the reality of growing income inequality evidenced by cascading Gini coefficients[10] sparking spreading populist

---

[10] An economic measure of individual differences in income normalized on a scale of zero (perfect equality) to one (perfect inequality). In recent years, America's Gini coefficient has been trending higher and higher.

movements across the globe. In the United States and around the world, people are finally starting to see past the poorly constructed facade.

This has resulted in a series of movements — Black Lives Matter, Occupy Wall Street, and the Women's March, among others — aimed at addressing structural and historical inequalities. These endeavors are noble and necessary. They highlight hidden privilege, help to chip away at longstanding injustices, and ultimately make the world a more inclusive and harmonious place.

But one must also recognize a painful additional fundamental truth — namely, that you have no choice but to play the hand you are dealt.

This is what my grandfather taught me by making the most out of his limited resources. He was a man born in British occupied India, ultimately rising meteorically to join the Supreme Court of an independent India.

I believe that every person's particular set of circumstances — race, gender, income, family, and so forth — lends itself to a grab bag. Inside of this grab bag, you will find both positives and negatives.

Sure, some people will have a more limited grab bag than others. Others will find their grab bag populated almost entirely with positives.

But nobody will find their grab bag entirely devoid of a singular positive.

In my case, there are obvious negatives. On balance, these include more "random" airport screenings and a general level of distrust in public settings. But I would be remiss to gloss over the phenomenal positives my grab bag has granted me.

For instance, as a brown skinned person I can travel the world without raising eyebrows. While a white or black person would be instantly profiled, I can travel anywhere without calling unwanted attention to myself.

Moreover, as a man, I can go anywhere without tangible fear for my body. This is something my female compatriots will likely never have the privilege of experiencing, but which I get to benefit from simply by virtue of the grab bag I was granted at birth.

At the end of the day, we have to make the most out of our respective grab bags. We have to embrace the hand that we are dealt, because no amount of groveling can change it.

My grandfather did it throughout his life. Despite losing his mother at a very young age and growing up in a colonial state where he was definitionally disadvantaged, he went on to become the youngest High Court Judge in India's to-date history before subsequently being elevated to the Supreme Court. Not once did he use perceived – or, in his case actual – victimhood as a crutch to prevent him from attaining the success he so desired.

I don't know the full story behind the homeless man at *Sbarro's* and how he got to that point, but in some narrowly tailored way, he too made the made the most of his grab bag to find a meal — at least on that particular day. And everyone must strive to do the same, each and every day of their lives.

Understand this, however.

Optimizing your grab bag doesn't mean accepting life as it is. As Gandhi famously declaimed, you must still fight for the change you wish to see. Our hope is that each individual grab bag becomes a less important predictor of success with each passing generation because that will mean that the egalitarian dream is being realized, however slowly it may be.

But you must also strive forward to make the life that you were given better — even if you start off with an inferior grab bag. That entails a sober acceptance of the reality of your circumstances and a firm commitment to stave off adversity for the sake of your own improvement. After all, pointing out that the rules of the race are unfair and winning the race do not have to be mutually exclusive pursuits.

For those of us who are more fortunate, such as myself, there is a different responsibility.

We must constantly take up the mantle to fight for those whose grab bags aren't quite so well stocked. And, most importantly, we must possess the humility to recognize and check our privilege whenever we think we have it tough.

Chapter 6:
The spirit of the law

December 14-15, 2013
Moscow, Russia → St. Petersburg, Russia

The post-prandial period inexorably fosters a heightened sense of fatigue, often served with a concomitant side of somnolence. But when in Russia, nap time can always wait for the train.

We stuffed our knapsacks and readied ourselves to head back out into the crisp, frigid Moscow air. The next stop on our list — Red Square. The jewel in the crown of the plaza is St. Basil's Cathedral.

Since 1561, this magnificent building has blessed the Moscow skyline. It is a kaleidoscopic feast for the senses. Bright, fluorescent colors accost the viewer and nullify all else around it. In a country that can at times feel dreary, if not distinctly lifeless, St. Basil's Cathedral feels singularly out of place — akin to an avuncular septuagenarian lounging in the waiting room of a pediatrician's office.

Instantly, I knew it belonged firmly in the ranks of the top five sights I've seen in my lifetime.

I fixated on its beauty, silently chiding the thousands of pedestrians walking by who lacked my palpable sense of entrancement while purposely ignoring the reality that they had probably seen it thousands of times prior. Seconds turned to minutes, and it became exceedingly difficult to pry my eyes away from the ornately crafted towers that rose to the sky, symbolizing a bonfire with its mysterious embers rising upwards to the heavens.

When I finally shifted my gaze, I noted with more bemusement than alarm that Avi was missing.

"No worries," I thought. "He must have gone around to get a better view and take some more pictures."

Ten minutes passed, and I parked myself on a nearby bench.

Still no sign of Avi.

I ventured back into the heart of the square to look for him.

As my eyes scanned the surroundings, I spotted my fellow traveler struggling to communicate with a police officer and holding his phone out limply in front of his skinny body. I did not desire another confrontation with the authorities after my experience the previous night, so I observed from a safe distance to avoid inflaming the situation. A couple more minutes elapsed before Avi was granted permission to walk away, phone still sheepishly extended in hand.

"Dude, what happened?" I asked.

"Nothing, man. I took a picture of him and he made me delete it."

Avi quickly took a furtive glance over his shoulder, recognized that the officer was not looking, and speedily snapped another photo of him.

"You're a fool," I chuckled to myself. "Let's go."

We meandered through the square and snaked through the GUM department store, a building with an eight-hundred-foot facade and a gorgeous glass dome — the epitome of high class. It did not take long for our ragtag American crew, exhibiting all the classic characteristics of a parvenu, to be summarily outed as impostors.

After the brief respite from the cold, we worked our way back outside and slalomed through a festive Christmas market in the middle of the square.

There was a certain vibrancy to this scene, resplendent with Disney ice sculptures, prize booths, and games for the family. It was a side of Russia that we would be hard-pressed to encounter again — one of unabashed smiles and laughs, the literal antithesis of the moroseness the country is so famed for.

While I could have spent several more hours here in the Square, I knew we had to catch our train to St. Petersburg. Dusk fell, and we headed to the train station to begin our journey of a thousand plus miles, all the while queueing the Vanessa Carlton soundtrack in our minds.

After brief confusion surrounding our ticket numbers, we located our carriage — one that we had all to ourselves — and boarded the train to St. Petersburg. While Avi and I had years of experience riding Indian sleeper train carriages, Jeremy was utterly blown away by the compartment, irrupting into unmitigated, stream-of-consciousness laudation.

"These trains have beds? We can go to sleep? How are you guys so calm?" he shouted, desperately seeking affirmation.

"Everyone should travel like this!"

Suffice to say, one hundred hours of subsequent train time would slightly alter his opinion.

The journey had begun.

Lesson

Once upon a time in Peru, I traveled to the traditional Incan historical site of Moray. At the gate, I asked for the student admission fee and presented my Duke ID. The lady behind the counter examined the card and handed it back.

"This isn't valid," she said. "You must pay the full price."

"Excuse me?" I responded. "Hold on. I can prove that I am a student."

I pulled out my phone and showed the gatekeeper several pieces of corroborating evidence, including but not limited to: class emails, a document of enrollment, and a notice of upcoming graduation.

"It doesn't matter," she stubbornly insisted. "The ID doesn't have a graduation date on it, so it is invalid. You do not qualify for the student discount."

On the path back down the mountain I fumed openly, tacitly inviting Jeremy to jump into the fray.

"She was just doing her job, man," he said. "Stop being so hard on her."

"No way!" I retorted. "The point of the discount is to incentivize student visits by letting them in for cheaper. She followed the rules, but she violated the spirit of the law!"

I am firmly of the belief that laws are, and should always be guidelines. Outside of family, there is almost nothing in life that should carry the firm rigidity of permanency.

In *99 Problems*, when Jay-Z was pulled over by the police for "doing fifty-five in a fifty-four" — going one mile per hour over the speed limit — he unquestionably broke the law. But should he have been stopped?

Hardliners may say yes, but I would argue a resounding no. Insofar as that is the case, I believe that we should grant a certain level of leeway in the application of all laws, especially if they result in outcomes that are unequal or unintended. In the Netherlands, a legal term exists specifically for this phenomenon.

They call it *gedogen*.

Gedogen is the idea that while a law may exist, it need not always be stringently enforced. Two conditions must meet to satisfy the *gedogen* criteria. First, it must be incredibly difficult to enforce the law equally amongst all parties. Second, violation of the law must not cause undue duress to society.

The Dutch apply this principle largely to paternalistic laws. That is why in Amsterdam, for instance, you can smoke marijuana.

Marijuana prohibition cannot be equally enforced — while you may catch one person toking up because you monitor his crime-laden neighborhood more closely, you consequently turn a blind eye to the rich college student doing just the same. Moreover, the smoking activity of one individual is not a net harm to society. Indeed, it is largely inconsequential to the rest of us. Thus, pot usage falls under the protective umbrella of *gedogen*.

It isn't technically legal — its illegality simply goes unenforced.[11]

And such should have been the case with the student discount policy. The guidelines were set with the intention of excluding non-students from taking advantage of a program intended to incentivize youth visits. Since the harshness of the guidelines resulted in actual students being barred, there should have been some leeway for the authority in charge to determine who met the criteria independent of the rules.

There is a tradeoff between openly flouting authority and blindly following the rules. A life of critical self-examination is necessarily a life in which one constantly questions why things are as they are.

That's why I love the fact that Avi took a picture of the officer.

He made a calculation that his picture did not cause harm to the community but brought him personal enjoyment by establishing a memory. He took the snap in a respectful manner by doing so in secret, and he was prepared to deal with the fallout of that decision.

Likewise, Russia has a good reason to bar people from taking pictures of officers. Surely they don't want those pictures in the hands of people who wish to do evil to police officers.

---

11   To me, this is the best potential outcome. The state does not condone or incentivize the activity, but it removes itself from making the situation worse.

Those two ideas can co-exist, and both sides can come out feeling like winners. As with many things in life, this doesn't have to be a zero-sum game — though it may feel like one.

In life, one must question rules, but do so respectfully and thoughtfully. If a rule is nonsensical, and if breaking it causes no harm to the community but actively benefits the rule-breaker — and moreover, if doing so is just — then why not break it?

Take another example. At Duke, slots for classes were limited by registration status. Sometimes, simply by virtue of having a lower Internet speed, I would be unable to sign up for courses I wanted to take before they filled up.

Rather than submitting to those rules, I simply showed up for the classes I wanted to take, even if I was not officially registered. I stayed long enough that the professors ended up letting me enroll in their classes, each and every time. It was a testament not only to persistence, but to intelligent rule-breaking. Had I followed the letter of the law, I am convinced that my college experience would have been far less fulfilling.

Before you get the wrong idea, though, let me be clear. I am by no means an anarchist.

I believe in laws and institutions and in their fundamental importance in keeping society functional and productive. As a former resident of Seattle, I saw firsthand the destruction that lawlessness caused every May Day, so I have no sympathy for wanton insouciance. I am, after all, the grandson of a lawyer-turned-judge.

Nonetheless, I do sometimes break rules. And sometimes I break conventions.

But only in the narrowly tailored context wherein it is justified — namely, when it causes harm to none, and gain to some. And I wholeheartedly assume the risks that go along with that.

So far in life, doing so has treated me just fine.

Chapter 7: Who decides what is offensive?

December 15, 2013
St. Petersburg, Russia

The overnight train to St. Petersburg was largely uneventful.

This would be the first and only time on the trip that we traveled westward, and, as such, some of the mystique of the journey was lost on this leg. Moreover, the three of us were wrecked from a long day of exploration in Moscow, according the perfect opportunity for unencumbered rest en route to our destination.

Avi and I slept the entire way, waking up just slightly before entering the city. Jeremy, still giddy from his first train experience, stayed up almost all night. Perversely, the delightful shock of the comfort of sleeper carriage travel prevented him from falling asleep — the very activity that he desired.

While I couldn't resist the opportunity to poke fun at him for this, I must admit to my own hypocrisy. Just the year before, on an *Emirates* flight from Kozhikode to Dubai, I was surreptitiously upgraded to first class for free. Not understanding Malayalam, the native language, I heard my name over the PA system but was devoid entirely of context. Fearing a problem with my reservation, I was surprised and delighted when a flight attendant walked me to my seat at the front of the aircraft and handed me a glass of champagne before takeoff.

Being my first experience riding in first class on an international flight, I fought desperately to stay awake so as not to waste any perceived value. But unlike Jeremy, I nodded off in my fully reclining airline seat just minutes into the flight in spite of my valiant attempts to the contrary.

As we approached St. Petersburg, the task of attempting to decipher the correct station to disembark generated a frisson of excitement amongst the group. Most large cities host more than one train station, and St. Petersburg proved no exception to the rule — so we had a choice on our hands.

We opted, rather blindly, for the second city stop. The winning argument posited that at least there was a nearby McDonald's through which we could reliably bank on a free Wi-Fi connection to get ourselves oriented in the correct direction to our hostel. Once on the network, a quick Google Maps search demonstrated that we had indeed miscalculated. There was another station closer to home.

Unfazed, we routed to the nearest subway station and boarded a line towards the main street of St. Petersburg — Nevsky Prospekt — near where our hostel, self-deprecatingly named *Party Train*, was located. Upon emerging from the depths of the station, we were forced to avoid black ice, a deluge of pedestrians, cars parked in all manner of circumstance (including on the sidewalk), and even a singular falling heroin needle from a high-rise apartment.

Seeking respite and warmth, we ducked off the main road into an alleyway where a small village-like structure emerged replete with shops offering cornucopias of bread and cheese. After some brief navigational difficulties, including an accidental entry into a private home and several near stumbles, we located the sign to our hostel and entered.

"Welcome to *Party Hostel*," offered the man behind the front desk in a tone so blithely ambivalent as to be almost comical. "Passports, please."

This is standard procedure for any hostel visit, and a guarantor of dead time as the host inevitably excuses himself to take a photocopy of the identification. Before he had the chance to do so, I figured I would capitalize on the opportunity by inquiring to use the restroom.

The man took one look at me up and down, fixating on my afro hair, before serving up an off-color remark accompanied by a dry smile.

"You are a criminal?" he asked.

The comment hit me like a blow.

I staggered, disoriented and logy, merely offering a stammered, "Wait. . . what?" in response.

The man asked again, with a tinge more seriousness this time around.

"Criminal?"

"Uh... nah," I spitballed.

He pointed in the direction of the restroom, and I stumbled over to ease myself, still reeling from the weight of the comment. As I stood in the restroom, I ruminated endlessly on what had just transpired.

Could it be chalked up merely to a classic case of Russian humor[12] gone bad? Was I at fault for my dour attitude? As Gertrude Stein would offer, was there simply no there there?

Or rather, was there something there? Something more insidious behind what the man had just said to me?

I was conflicted.

The exchange had made me upset — but more so it made me angry. How could a stranger who had just met me have the temerity — the unmitigated gall — to make such a comment?

And yet, I had to balance the countervailing truth of the matter.

This was a culture I did not quite understand yet. What had just transpired could merely have been an innocuous comment, just as likely to have been offered to white Jeremy as it was to me. I had just happened to set myself up for it, was all.

Racking my brain, I couldn't remember a time in my life growing up in the melting pot that is the San Francisco Bay Area where I had been so much as cognizant of any sense of discomfort associated with my "minority" status.

But now, in this moment, it felt real.

Nonetheless, I resolved to linger on it no longer. After all, Russia wouldn't be Russia without the occasional pangs of discomfort.

---

12   Several Russians attempted to describe the concept of 'Russian humor' to us over the course of the trip, but I must admit that I never fully grasped it. To this day, I am convinced that it is a catch-all phrase to describe any joke or interaction that does not land well – so if there is anything in this book that confuses you, let me be the first to tell you it's just 'Russian humor.'

Lesson

There is a debate raging these days.

It pivots quite firmly along generational lines. Nevertheless, it would be silly to reduce it to merely a case of cranky "get-off-my-lawn" behavior.

There is, indeed, some merit in this criticism. And there is some worth in this conversation.

The idea is that the younger generation — millennials, as we are colloquially known — is too sheltered. Our world is one of echo chambers and political correctness, the argument goes. Our cohort as a whole has become "softer" for it. We are caricatured as "snowflakes", looking for safe spaces — lost souls, incapable of engaging in the rigors of substantive, character-building, intellectual debate.

The claim is not entirely baseless.

In fact, it is the beginning of some truth. It is indeed easier, in an age of ubiquitous technology, to stay in one's own bubble and to avoid confronting uncomfortable ideas. And surely, many millennials do retreat into a sort of victimhood mentality to shield themselves from taking adequate and complete responsibility for their own incompetencies.

But there is a certain insidiousness behind those bigots and racists who hide underneath the veneer of avoiding political correctness merely as a guise behind which to deflect criticism of their own unacceptably intolerant vitriol. Millennials who show zero tolerance for this type of behavior — name calling, denial of basic human rights, and blatant disrespect — are not "snowflakes."

Rather, they are courageous — demonstrating wisdom and fortitude far beyond their years.

When I was in college at Duke, I was part of a collective social co-op living group called Mirecourt. Our group, like most others on campus, had an active and lively email listserv. On one particular occasion, a message was sent out with a free form response tool included for the purpose of allowing readers to suggest new colors to paint the bench outside of our dormitory. One of the responses was "Asian colored."

Was this response insensitive? Or was it simply a joke — potentially in poor taste, but entirely harmless nonetheless?

It seemed, for the most part, that majority opinion erred towards the latter. That is, until a member of the group — let's call her Tiffany — emailed back the following response.

"So, would someone like to explain to me what an Asian colored bench would look like? I'm really not understanding how my skin tone (if that is what this person is referring to) and my culture are being reduced to a color for our fucking bench."

Was Tiffany a typical liberal snowflake? Did she need to toughen up? Was she symptomatic of this larger problem within our generation?

Or did she have a right to be upset?

A debate raged on the list-serv.

Many members — predominantly white and male — argued that the joke was nothing more than that. While they showed sympathy for Tiffany's position, they urged her to lighten up and insisted that what she perceived as offensive simply was not. If she were truly a friend of the group, she would understand that her cohabitants hadn't meant to denigrate her cruelly.

I will never forget the response of another member – the group's President, and also a white male – who we'll call Marcus. His message ended the thread.

"If someone is offended then it's offensive," he replied to the thread. "It's in the eye of the recipient. 'Being friends' means the ability to rectify and move past issues amicably."

I generally perceive myself as someone who is largely unaffected by criticism. I find precious little offensive, and I do not take affront to potentially insensitive talk as a general rule. Moreover, I personally did not find the "Asian colored" comment particularly odious or repulsive in the way that Tiffany did.

But I still found a beautiful kernel of wisdom contained in Marcus's words.

Not everyone shares your feelings. Just because you are not personally offended by something does not mean that it is not offensive.

Nobody wants to live in a world where we must walk on eggshells trying to avoid hurting each other's feelings. But we should want to live in a world where we can recognize that our words carry different meanings to different peoples. And, at the very least, we should all be willing to demonstrate some modicum of effort to respect those alternative viewpoints.

Most importantly, we should live in a world where we aren't too proud to apologize when we hurt those feelings — even, and actually most crucially, when we didn't intend to do so in the first place.

Chapter 8:
Head on a swivel

December 15, 2013
St. Petersburg, Russia

After checking in at the hostel, the three of us threw our bags down, caught our respective breaths, and prepared to hit the town. We had booked a twenty-four bed room — a classic budget traveler maneuver to save money.

But the room was empty.

It soon became apparent that the three of us would be the sole residents of the *Party Train*. I felt like Shane Smith, President of *VICE Media*, on his inaugural trip to North Korea.[13]

"All of this, just for us?"

Either other backpackers weren't going to be duped by the *Party Train*, or only fools would suffer Russia in the winter. Perhaps, more accurately, the truth lay somewhere in between.

Nevertheless, I couldn't complain. A capacious living environment for the night could be the perfect antidote for the spirits after a rough evening constrained within a minuscule train compartment. We stopped to shower briefly — a cathartic necessity, given the physical and emotional weight of the trip and the events that had just occurred — and suited up to head into the city.

Our first stop of the day was the Palace Square. Within its borders lies the Winter Palace, abode of the Russian royals from the eighteenth to twentieth centuries.

---

13   In a gripping documentary, Smith visits a hotel in North Korea only to realize that all the pomp and pageantry associated with the stay is merely a show entirely put on for him – the singular guest.

The building marks the spot of the genesis of the Bolshevik Revolution, an event that would shape Russia and the geopolitical universe forever. On these grounds, the world witnessed the genesis of the Communist experiment. The magnitude of what transpired here is not lost in the twenty-first century, as evidenced by the meteoric rise of China — perhaps today's pre-eminent world force, and almost inexorably tomorrow's.

The Winter Palace has managed to maintain a resplendent aura of luminescent beauty — a feat made all the more remarkable by the reality of a past defined by turmoil and turbulence, and a present marred by the lugubrious backdrop of gray skies and ubiquitous ice. Its rectangular facade extends almost one thousand feet long and one hundred feet high, ensconced in a shroud of minty green and white, and lined with nearly two thousand doors. The building overlooks the Neva River, completely frozen over for the season. Walking through the square, it is not hard to imagine Tsar Nicolas[14] inside a study, watching his children gallivant outside, blissfully ignorant of his incipient fate.

I stopped and took in the scene. This halcyon setting, so unperturbed on the inside, with the energy of the ghosts of history's past — the unbecoming site of a grisly and world-changing revolution.

After a couple of hours roaming the square and perambulating through the palace — inside of which exists a collection of classic artwork from some of history's finest artists — we headed out en route to the Church of the Savior on Spilled Blood. This landmark is seen as St. Petersburg's analogue to Moscow's St. Basil's Cathedral.

Indeed, in many ways it is markedly reminiscent of the latter with its five domed, brilliantly colored facade and gorgeous interior. It has a history to match, with its interior having been ransacked and nearly destroyed by the Bolsheviks during the revolution.

Yet to me, the building seemed gaudy to the point of garish — showy to the point of ostentatious. I intend in no way to impugn what is undoubtedly one of the world's great architectural accomplishments — to each their own. I merely submit my preference for

---

14 Perhaps less well-known than his daughter Anastasia who was featured in an eponymous Disney animation, Tsar Nicholas II met a bloody end when the Bolsheviks captured power in the early 20th century.

St. Basil's Cathedral — a building that, to my mind, most remarkably straddles the fine line between brazen and beautiful.

After exploring the premises of the church, we crossed the street to visit a traditional outdoor Russian market. We encountered a shambolic series of stalls offering all sorts of sundry counterfeit and makeshift goods, from handbags to vodka shot glasses. Each of the vendors were attired in *ushankas*, the Russian fur caps with flaps over the ears that are iconically associated with the country's brutally cold winters.

For the typical outsider, such a market could be an obvious pratfall — a brazen tourist trap.

But I had hardened myself with previous market experiences ranging from Mexico to Morocco, and Guatemala to Zimbabwe. I understood the "game" that was to be played. A friendly offer of "a good deal" was always to be accompanied by a healthy dose of mendacity. The key was to stand firm, stick to your guns, and bargain hard.

Merchants naturally look for any advantage they can elicit over a buyer, and they had an obvious one. It was a dead giveaway that we weren't Russian — we were playing on their turf.

But I also had an advantage — namely, the mystery of my background.

Sellers seek to establish trust in a buyer, making it easier to dupe them into overpayment. Yet in order to do this, communication is key. By virtue of my ethnically ambiguous features, it wasn't easy to gauge my nationality — and, subsequently, to know my language. You only get one chance to make a first impression, and attempting to communicate in the wrong tongue is a dagger in the heart of a potential sale.

I watched the strain on the vendors' faces as they read my features and attempted to communicate with me. Attempts to establish a rapport were met with stoic and blank stares of ostensible confusion. The languages flowed as I walked by stalls.

Russian, Arabic, Hindi, Swahili, and English.

I stopped for nothing, and didn't say a word to Avi or Jeremy. Hearing us speak smooth English in an American accent would be the most mellifluous sound a vendor could hope for, ensuring tenfold price markups on any potential acquisition. I was not about to play the role of the "dumb" American and make their jobs easier for them.

After a while meandering, I found a chess set I wished to purchase at a booth manned by a pretty brunette Russian woman in an intimidating fur hat. I spoke in heavily broken English, and, upon inquiry, indicated falsely that I was from Brazil. This traditionally is my default modus operandi, and it has been a successful one for three reasons.

First, Portuguese is not widely spoken in many locales and hence, few are able to fact check my backstory. Second, indicating that you are from Brazil rather than America lends itself to better pricing because of the corresponding assumption that you are not quite as wealthy. Finally, my hair and skin tone naturally corroborate my story without undue suspicion.

"How much?" I asked.

"Two thousand rubles," she offered.

I laughed uproariously.

"Two hundred. At most."

"No, it is of great quality my friend!" she pleaded.

I shook my head, shrugged my shoulders, made an about-face, and walked away.

"Wait!" she said, chasing me out of the booth. "I'll give you special student discount. Five hundred, just for you!"

I turned around, gave it a semblance of thought, shook my head, and skulked away once more.

"Fine! Two hundred! Here!" she opined in desperation as she scrambled to bag the set and run it over towards me.

I walked back to the stall, paid the cash, and acquired my set.

In all likelihood, the fact that the woman so readily agreed to the price suggests that I paid more than the chess board was worth. But at the end of the day, negotiation is about setting the price you feel the product is worth and paying only that.

I felt like the chess set was easily worth the equivalent of four American dollars, and so I left gleefully. And if I overpaid a bit, it went to a hard-working merchant who likely needed the money more than me. Life doesn't need to consist exclusively of zero-sum games, and everyone wins when nobody feels cheated.

After Jeremy and Avi acquired their respective market trinkets, we met up contentedly and made plans to head to the world-renowned Mariinsky Theatre. We are by no means opera heads.

Indeed, even the remote implication that we are would likely be anathema to true aficionados. But, we figured, "when in Russia, do as the Russians do."

Sadly, the only available show at the time was Madame Butterfly, a show that cost a pretty penny at over one hundred dollars per ticket. And so we defaulted to the plan of action that any price-sensitive college student would, calling an audible and heading for the nearest food and drinks spot. The restaurant we settled upon was a quirky Chinese spot with a wholly unsettling vibe. Sitting down at the booth with Tsingtaos in hand gave us some time to reflect on the absurdity of the situation.

Our group of three multicultural Americans were in Russia in the middle of winter eating at a Chinese restaurant with various tributes to Mao and Communism in a setting more out of the Cultural Revolution of the 1970s than the dawn of 2014. After munching on some fried rice and bok choy, we showed ourselves the door with alacrity and headed for the city.

Rather than walking for an hour in the cold, we resolved to use public transit to get back to the hostel. After a series of stultified inquiries with bemused passerby on the street, we figured out the proper on-boarding location and waited for the bus.

Upon embarking, Avi attempted to hand the conductor the precise fare. Clearly frustrated by our ignorance and limited by his inability to explain the proper protocol without holding up a busload of work weary Russians, he grumpily hand-waved us to the back of the bus at no cost. Given the crowded nature of the vehicle, the three of us huddled near a back-exit door.

We strained our eyes out onto the street, catching the night lights of St. Petersburg and trying desperately to figure out the right location on Nevsky Prospekt to disembark. At one of the first stops, there was a wild commotion as two men pushed their way through us to get off, ostensibly in a hurry.

In the chaos, Avi was tossed off the bus and onto the street. Concerned, we called out to the conductor to leave the door open for Avi to re-board. He managed to fight his way back through the crowd onto the bus.

"What happened, man?" I asked.

"They went for my wallet. I held onto it, though."

An impish foreign man[15] (sorry, Avi) on the back of a bus near an exit door makes a prime target for a pickpocketing attempt. Luckily for him, he had the wherewithal to keep his hand on his pocket during the strong-arming and to exit the vehicle along with the attempted robbers. The criminals fled on foot and escaped into the night, but what could have been an awful experience vaporized into nothing more than an innocuous learning moment for the group.

Awakened by the night's events, we got off at our subsequent stop with more awareness and clarity of mind than ever before and headed back to the hostel to make plans for the evening. We were rattled, but undeterred.

After all, the real trip was yet to begin.

---

15   As an author, there is a natural tension between presenting the details as objectively as possible and considering the feelings of the individuals involved in description. In this case, I have opted to prioritize the former. Apologies to the imp – though in fairness, my categorization is far more generous than that of the Moroccan street vendors who referred to him as a "skinny wanker."

Lesson

Recently, I was perusing a real estate website and found a two-bedroom apartment in the South of Market district of San Francisco for two thousand dollars per month.

In most locales, that sum would be preposterous. But in arguably the most expensive city in the world, it was a steal of unmatched proportions. Indeed, comparable apartments in that location — near the San Francisco Giants ballpark and the Caltrain station — generally went for double the price.

Excited but skeptical, I reached out to the ostensible seller with a phone call. There was no response, but a few minutes later I received a text.

"Hello, this is James Johnson. You are interested in the unit on King Street. When is your intended move in date? How long do you plan to lease this unit?"

Normal questions so far, to which I delivered the appropriately reciprocal quotidian responses.

"The unit will be ready for viewing in two weeks," James said. "In the meantime, please provide the following information: name, location, move in date, occupation, and email."

The lack of immediate availability for touring elicited some doubt, so I decided to give the seller another phone call. This time, he picked up. A good omen indeed — but I resolved to let the content of the conversation dictate whether or not my concerns would be fully allayed.

"Since you are the first person who reached out, I wanted to give you the opportunity to buy first," James said. "You cannot visit the apartment until the fifteenth, but it looks exactly like the pictures. You can put down the security deposit now and then view it after the 15th. If you do not like the unit, I will return the amount in full."

At this point, the full-blown ruse became overwhelmingly obvious. The classic tenets of a scam artist were readily apparent — making the buyer feel special, insisting on the quality without allowing for viewership, heading straight for the cash, and issuing a no-strings-attached money-back guarantee.

But I was feeling amused, so I decided to play along with James.

"That sounds phenomenal," I replied via text. "Send the lease details over to my email. I am super excited!"

Unable to contain his giddiness, James immediately emailed over a document that looked like a traditional lease agreement — that is, except for one glaring red flag. A line in the document read, "make the order out to 'FiveZero International Bank.'"

Hadn't heard of that one in my life. Neither had Google.

The next day, I received a follow-up text from James.

"Have you made a decision on the apartment yet?" he inquired.

"Yes!" I responded, feigning enthusiasm. "I have wired the money to FiveZero. Shall we talk now to discuss logistics?"

Radio silence from James for the next twenty-four hours. That is, until the next day when I got another text.

"The money has not arrived yet," he noted. "Can you try sending it again? After that, I will call you to discuss move-in logistics over the phone."

I sent James one final correspondence. A string of laughing emojis. ":-):-):-):-):-):-):-):-):-)"

Turns out, the player had just gotten played.

Sadly, the reality is that not all of these stories end in laughter — in fact, far too many of them end in tears.

And the old adage continues to hold true. If it seems too good to be true, it almost certainly is.

Though this world is filled with myriad examples of love and kindness, it is imperative to constantly be on your toes. Some people — they tend, overwhelmingly, to be Nigerian princes — will look to take advantage of the weak or to wheedle the gullible. This is a perverse form of social Darwinism at its very worst, and it often puts the most trusting and benevolent amongst us at the most risk of harm.

At the end of the day, whether you are bargaining in a night market or evading pickpockets on public transit, you must remember to look out for yourself. Nobody else owes you that responsibility.

Be a natural skeptic. Ask a ton of questions. Don't divulge your hand without compelling reason. And take your time before making decisions. Being patient and probing rather than impetuous and accepting can save a lot of heartache and prevent irreversible errors.

But most importantly, know that the panacea is not to give up the faith.

Never stop believing in innate human kindness. I saw much more of it on my trip and in my life than I have seen of evil, as I will discuss in more depth later.

Be guarded, but open. Be careful, but not fearful. You will find that doing so will help you not only to steer clear of the bad, but also to appreciate all that is good.

Chapter 9:
Keep it trill

December 15-16, 2013
St. Petersburg, Russia

We re-entered the hostel if not ebulliently, at least with a certain extra bounce in our step.

While failure is enervating, there is something particularly enlivening about just nearly avoiding it. In the case of Avi's attempted wallet snatch, we all felt that we had dodged a bullet — he because his financials were safe, and us because the photos we knew we would rely upon for the trip were still in his firm, if unsafe and tiny hands.

Avi had scooped up a fifth of Russian Standard vodka on the route back, and we cracked it open to loosen up a bit before heading out on the town for the night. The *Party Train* seemed an appropriate venue for such an activity on an early evening in St. Petersburg. Yet strangely, we were the only inhabitants awake and active at the relatively benign hour of 8:00 PM.

Our conversation ranged over many topics.

We discussed the fortune and privilege of attending one of the top ten universities in America, and how it had lent itself to internship opportunities providing the means of accumulating the cash necessary to make this trip. We spoke of the absurdity of where we were. And we basked in the moment, noting that our future married selves would never be able to drag a spouse to a trip in Russia — so while our friends Instagrammed photos from Paris, we knew that France could wait for some distant day in the future.

As the minutes passed, we continued laughing and drinking merrily. I asked Jeremy to take another shot of vodka. He summarily refused, to which I immediately — and frankly, in an almost conditioned manner — retorted, "oh, don't be a bitch!"

"See, that's a word I don't use anymore," he responded.

"Why not?" I asked. "You swear like a sailor, and all of a sudden you don't like curse words?"

I scoffed at the seeming hypocrisy of his statement.

"Nah, man. I don't think there's anything wrong with swearing," he offered. "It's just that there are some words that are offensive to certain groups of people that I don't think we should ever really use."

Often pugilistic and impetuous, a deadly combination when it comes to verbal debates, I fired back.

"I mean, if you're going to be consistent then you should stop saying all swear words," I shot back defensively. "The word 'fuck' might be offensive to some people, but you say it all the fucking time!"

Jeremy paused thoughtfully, before positing a clear response.

"I think it's different, man," he said softly. "Fuck is offensive to everyone, but it isn't particularly offensive to a certain group. I don't have an issue with swearing, but it's the discriminatory words that I try to cut out of my vocabulary."

You know that feeling when you're in the wrong but you hate to admit it so you keep trying to make a sinking ship float? That was me.

"Well, obviously context matters," I said. "I would never say that word with women around because it may be offensive. But when it's just the two of you, it's different. You know what I meant."

I looked at Avi longingly, hoping for support. He shrugged.

"Honestly, man, I agree with Jeremy. There are enough curse words out there that don't marginalize whole groups of people that we can use."

I sighed. It was true.

They were right, and a person must possess the humility to acknowledge when they are wrong. I had to resign.

"Alright, fair comment," I offered, relenting a bit. "You still need to take your shot though, you fuck!"

We all laughed and took another shot. The conversation continued for a while until we were rudely interrupted by the hostel staff.

"Excuse me, no drinking in the hostel."

The three of us looked at the woman incredulously.

Jeremy asked, "There's no drinking in the *Party Train*?"

"*Nyet.*"

No.

Slightly bemused, but not particularly upset, we wrapped up the session and headed out onto the street. Drinking had reset our appetites and the Chinese food had not particularly hit the spot, so we ducked into a small family restaurant for a quick bite of pierogi.

The shop owner instantly took a peculiar interest in the three of us.

"America!" he shouted. "I have always wanted to go."

The man struck us as earnest without being smarmy. He entertained us throughout the meal. We smiled and laughed and felt a connection. I enjoyed the company, and more importantly the food — which was absolutely scrumptious.

When it came time to pay the bill, the man said, "Ah, since you have been great friends, I will give you a special discount."

"Oh, it's fine!" we replied. "The food was great. We must pay the full price."

Looking at the menu, which was hung in plain sight, the total cost came out to somewhere in the twelve-to-fifteen-dollar range — totally reasonable for what we had just consumed.

"Oh, but I insist!" he persisted. "I will give you a special discount, my friends."

Gratified, we waited for the man to present the bill. But much to our chagrin, the number printed was more in the range of thirty-five dollars — well above what the menu had indicated.

Surely it must have been a misunderstanding — one that we assumed could be worked out quite easily.

"I think there must be some mistake," I said. "Look at the price on the menu — it's half of this. Maybe you mixed up our order with another party?"

"No, my friends," he responded. "I am giving you a discounted price. It is hard for me to explain because my English is quite poor, but trust me."

He hadn't had any trouble communicating with us until now. And while words may be different in Russian and English, the language of math is benevolently universal.

At this point, we realized that the man was just another snake oil salesman — that his exhortations of friendship amounted to nothing more than a ruse. A time-tested technique, a sales pitch meant to catch a sucker by surprise. I plopped my twelve dollars down on the table and headed for the exit.

"Wait, my friends, you have not paid enough!"

I turned around at the door, stared into the man's eyes, and responded.

"We have paid far too much. I am not your friend, and I am not a fool. Have a good night."

The experience left a poor taste in our mouths, but we escaped another money shaving scheme entirely unscathed. No harm, no foul.

For the next two hours, we roamed the icy streets of St. Petersburg without a singular destination in mind. This is my favorite activity in an unfamiliar city. I love to get lost in the mystery of a place, to experience the true culture of a community, and to have absolutely no conception of where I am at any given moment.

On our route, we passed kids playing in the snow, couples holding hands, drunks fighting on the sidewalk, and pimps pushing prostitutes. We saw majestic palaces of old, robust modern architecture, frozen ponds, and chic shops. But mostly, we encountered a place just like anywhere else.

A beautiful city full of people with lofty dreams and aspirations — some of whom were curious of the swarthy visitors aimlessly roaming their blocks, but most of whom paid no mind — living life and wondering simply where their feet would carry them next.

Lesson

Debate has always been a natural passion of mine.

In high school and for the first two years of college, I was a card-carrying member of my school's teams. I traveled, sometimes across states, to compete in tournaments — and quite often I won.

And yet, somewhere towards the end of my college career I began to lose interest. It's not that I had developed any level of frivolity towards the activity — in actuality, I still loved it. Rather, it's that I simply couldn't shake a fundamental, yet persistent perturbation with debate.

Namely: what was the point?

To rephrase running back Marshawn Lynch, who brushes a modern veneer over Sartre's time-tested existentialist philosophy — life is about actions, not words.

Don't talk about it. Be about it.

But perhaps the most insidious concern I had apropos the art of debate was the notion that one could stand publicly for something so adamantly, and yet privately detest the very opinion he spewed forth. Indeed, this was a necessity of debate itself.

And it bothered me.

If you were on the affirmative side, you had the luxury of bringing your own case to the table with your concomitant point of view behind it. But if you were assigned to the negative side — as you were, by definition, exactly half of the time — you were at the whims of your opponent as to which side of the debate you were required to fall on.

Sure, the burden of proof was on the affirmative, as outlined by the rules of the activity. But the burden of conscience was on you.

So if your opponents came into the room with a point of view that you wanted no part in opposing — say, for instance, they argued quite uncontroversially that the US policy of Japanese internment during World War II was cruel and unnecessary — you had only one of two options.

Argue for something anathema to your worldview, like the mass incarceration of thousands of innocent individuals solely on the basis of race.

Or forfeit. It was that simple.

Several months ago, the hacking collective Anonymous announced that it had obtained and would subsequently publish a list of names of current and former members of the Ku Klux Klan. In advance of the announcement, online trolls released spurious documents purporting to be the real deal.

Given the Internet's fierce reputation for populist vigilantism, it should be of no surprise that these fake lists spread like wildfire. They falsely indicted scores of innocent people.

There was a girl from Oakland — let's call her Sara — who I had debated against extensively throughout high school. Though I did not know her particularly well outside of the context of debate, I knew her well enough through the circuit and had followed her social media presence from afar.

I had respect for Sara. She was well-spoken and articulate, and she seemed like a person who believed in many of the same issues that I stood for. So I was not surprised when Sara posted one of the aforementioned lists of the persons allegedly implicated in the Anonymous KKK release on her personal Facebook. If in fact the list were genuine, these people did deserve our collective scorn.

But I knew the document that Sara posted was fabricated because I had done my research on it earlier in the day. In fact, I had learned that — among many other horror stories — a mom and pop store in Los Angeles was presently receiving innumerable death threats because it had been listed in the very fallacious report that Sara was now promulgating on Facebook.

The store was indeed named KK Mart. But those initials represented the first names of the two sons — Ken and Khoa — of a couple who had immigrated from Cambodia to Southern California at the height of the brutal Khmer Rouge regime. The store's acronym did not represent anything remotely relating to involvement with the Ku Klux Klan.

The spread of the fake list was causing irreparable harm to real people. So I decided to give Sara a heads-up by leaving a friendly comment on her Facebook post.

"I appreciate your desire to combat racism, but this list is actually a proven fabrication. Innocent people are being affected," I said, posting a link to the articles that corroborated this fact.

My expectation was that Sara would either respond acknowledging her error or delete the post to inhibit its spread and limit the damage.

Instead, she deleted my comment. And she kept the post.

I was floored.

But perhaps I shouldn't have been. Our generation is the first to have an open, digital forum allowing one to outwardly stand for issues that make one appear hip, cool or revolutionary, while inwardly possessing an utter disdain for those very same issues.

And that is why I believe — now more than ever — that it is so important to privately stand for what you publicly claim to believe in.

To be real. To be genuine.

And to not hide behind the hackneyed platitudes of your social media persona.

That night in St. Petersburg, I realized that I was being a phony. Privately using a word that demeans women while publicly proclaiming myself a feminist was wrong.

Party Train hostel was being phony. Privately limiting guest activities while publicly proclaiming itself to be a haven for backpacker fun was wrong.

And the restaurant owner was being a phony. Privately scheming to rip us off while publicly proclaiming to be a friend was wrong.

There was no other way around it.

There should be no disconnect between who we are privately and who we offer to the world publicly. We may act somewhat differently, and we may open up slightly differently — but our principles, at the very least, must remain steadfastly rock solid.

Ultimately, you may ask, "what's the big deal?" And sometimes, admittedly, it may not matter all that much.

But other times — as in the case of Sara — the juxtaposition between who you claim to be and who you actually are results in real negative consequences for the people you leave behind in your wake.

Don't be someone you're not.

Chapter 10: Solo star

December 16-17, 2013
St. Petersburg, Russia → Tyumen, Russia

I woke up the next morning in a *carpe diem*[16] mood — ready to seize the occasion.

It was our final day in St. Petersburg. More importantly, it was our last sunrise before the real trip would begin — the Trans-Siberian Railway.

St. Petersburg served as the western-most point on our journey. It was the kickoff node for an eight-thousand kilometer journey that would take us deep through Central Asia before ultimately depositing us in the Far East.

I, for one, was captivated by the city in a way that Moscow, while impressive, never managed to resonate with me. While no place in Russia can accurately be described as welcoming, St. Petersburg came the closest. And so I was grateful for an extra day in the relative comfort of this breathtaking city.

In life, humans tend to be suckers for reductionism. And so we cohort and collocate things into easily understandable buckets of myriad shapes and sizes.

Black and white. Big and small. Rich and poor. And so on and so forth.

And in the context of the world, we often talk of a generational and cultural clash between two competing lifestyles — that of the East, and that of the West.

But here lay St. Petersburg — a city defying rote classification, if not openly mocking it.

---

16   In Latin, "seize the day!" (Dead Poets Society, anyone?)

St. Petersburg stands at the nexus of these two countervailing geographic forces, an amalgamation of two distinct world-views that have slowly ground against one another for decades. It is a place that is constantly being tugged, and pushed, and pulled forth in all different directions — a tectonic flare waiting for a catalyst to combust.

Nonetheless, through all the years, it has steadfastly refused to pick a side — and it is all the better for it.

Moreover, St. Petersburg remains world-renowned as a haven for the intelligentsia. It is far from alone in that category. In the United States, the cities of Seattle — known for bookstores and coffee — and Boston — known for a confluence of universities — harbor similar reputations.

And yet, St. Petersburg actually lives up to its reputation in a way that most other places seem to fail. The aura about it is largely indescribable without one visiting and feeling the pulse of the streets. But as Justice Potter Stewart once famously quipped, while it may be hard to define, you almost certainly will "know it when [you] see it."[17]

And so it is with this careful mix of unbridled excitement, slight anxiety, and tempered veneration that I approached this ultimate day in St. Petersburg.

I spent much of it as I so often prefer to do, waking up early before Avi and Jeremy to amble around the streets outside of the *Party Train* alone. I walked up and down Nevsky Prospekt, ducked in and out of alleys, consumed copious amounts of bread at street stalls, and explored multiple bookstores along the way.

When I returned home, the whole crew was awake. We showered, got our minds right, and prepared to hit the streets one last time.

Avi offered that we head back to the Palace Square for a second visit. While I normally bristle at the suggestion of a repeat visit, be it to a place or a destination — why waste limited time on something that's already been seen when there's a swath of new places left to explore, I contend — I made a rare, but firm exception in this case. The Winter Palace was a magical destination and the square encapsulated what I loved about St. Petersburg — beauty, creativity, intellectualism, and the magical transient space where past meets present and one falls into an ephemeral dreamlike state just basking in its splendor.

---

17   Stewart, of course, was referencing pornography.

The walk to the Palace was filled with twists and turns, from falling icicles to street festivals. Upon arriving, I planted myself firmly in the middle of the square and reveled in its grandeur once more. I re-entered the building, appreciating the various artworks of Picasso, Monet, and Manet, among others. I walked out, headed to the outer facade of the building facing the water front, and hopped onto the connecting bridge.

For several minutes, I leaned over the railing, deep in thought and reflection. I watched the large pieces of frozen ice — captivating enough for a Californian kid encountering snow for the first time in his life — as they approached the undergirding of the bridge and crashed into tiny, disparate pieces.

Over and over and over again.

Schumpeter's famous cycle[18] was on full display — creation, disruption, and regeneration. The circle of life.

After spending many hours in the square, we only had time for a quick coffee and a brief sit-down supper before it was time to depart the city.

To my palate, Russian food was nothing to write home about — and that, perhaps, is why you have heard little of it thus far. But it was nevertheless comforting in the warmth and fullness it always seemed to provide. A cuisine, built over thousands of years, designed expressly to satisfy — but not to lend itself to excess. From an American perspective of overindulgence, there was something to appreciate in that ideal, if not the taste.

After dinner, we headed to the train station to commence our journey eastward. In this case, we did not have to deal with the hassle of trying to buy our train seats ourselves. I had previously arranged for this leg of the trip with an agency in London, and our tickets were already acquired — all the way through to Ulan Bator.

Yet the appearance of simplicity still proved largely a mirage. We arrived at the train station about twenty minutes before our allotted departure time and only managed to embark with about two minutes to spare — that too, only after a series of desperate gesticulations in the hopes of locating the correct platform and the proper carriage.

---

18   The Austrian born Joseph Schumpeter was famous for popularizing the notion of "creative destruction" – boom and bust – within the realm of economics.

At this point, the three of us found it necessary to establish some ground rules. If any of us were to miss a connection, we would simply have to arrange alternative plans to meet up in Ulan Bator.

Traveling together on this specific route, while important, was ancillary to the end goal of a united Mongolian Christmas. While we did not wish to lose each other, we were beginning to feel that this was a distinct possibility in a land of great uncertainty, zero communication, and phones lacking international data or calling capabilities.

We walked over to our compartment and found, once again, that despite our third-class status we had access to a comfortable sleeper with four beds. Unlike on our journey from Moscow to St. Petersburg, however, this compartment was to be shared with an unknown Russian traveler.

Jeremy and Avi quickly dove for the two beds on the opposite end of the compartment, leaving me on the side with our nameless Russian companion. Beat to the punch, I attempted to recover.

"OK, let's just rock, paper, scissors for the beds," I said. "It's the fairest way."

"Dude," Jeremy answered, "just shut up and take the third bed."

I sighed, tossed my bag next to my fellow traveler, and looked out of the window as the engine began to rumble, signifying the start of the Trans-Siberian railroad.

Eastward, ho!

Lesson

In the subsequent years following my trip to Russia, I have continued to backpack travel extensively. Among the motley assortment of questions I get asked, one presents itself to me with almost unfailing regularity.

"Do you prefer to travel with friends or to travel alone?"

The answer is difficult, because strict preference depends on a melange of different factors. On a trip to France, I'd far rather be with my girlfriend than alone. And on a trip to a natural park, I may very well rather be alone, lost in meaningful contemplation.

But there is one thing I know for certain: you have to be comfortable with either.

My reaction to being seated next to a random person was a poor one, but it was typical of myself at that stage in life. Indeed, it is typical of many, if not most young people. Of most people in general.

We seek refuge in familiarity. We actively avoid the unknown.

When I began my study abroad program at University College London a few months prior to the trip, I resolved to do it differently.

You see, I'd observed it before — the classic study-abroad mistake. American kids sign up to go to a different country, only to hang out with their same friends, engage with their own culture, and speak their same language.

Study abroad, USA.

So before I went, I promised myself this. When I got to England, I would force myself to hang out with new folks. My Duke friends would still be around when I returned to campus, but the memories I could make by putting myself outside of my comfort zone and meeting new people would be irreplaceable.

So when day one rolled around and my phone vibrated to the tune of Facebook notifications from my friends Jay and Benson to hang out, I ignored their familiar call. Instead, I went alone to International Student Orientation and I did the unthinkable.

I talked to the person next to me.

"Hey, where are you from?" I asked.

"Hi!" she responded smilingly. "I'm Rima. I'm from Berlin, Germany. And you?"

Rima remains my friend to this day, as do many others from that semester. More remarkably — so, too, do Jay and Benson.

And that is the amazing thing about friendships. If they're real, they will last.

With or without constant communication.

These days, social media has cultivated an atmosphere of constant FOMO — fear of missing out. We tend to use this term to describe the feeling of social anxiety that comes when our friends are out and about and we are not present with them.

But our real FOMO should come from missing out on opportunities that arise independently of our pre-existing friendships.

Recently, I had a conversation with one of my best friends from college, Yvette. I consider Yvette one of my five closest friends, but she certainly isn't one of the five people I talk to the most. That's for a variety of reasons — our lives are busy, we both stray largely away from social media, and we live in different cities now.

But when I'm in a bind, I know I can rely on Yvette to be there, and she on me. And moreover, the fact that I don't feel the need to constantly reach out to her to cement our friendship gives me confidence in the depth of our relationship.

Our friends should be a constant — people we can depend upon at all times. But new people and new experiences are few and far between. So when we get the opportunity to cultivate them, we should feel empowered to do so.

I moved back to the Bay Area recently after a couple of years working at Xbox in Seattle. At my new job, I started organizing pick-up basketball games to which I invited several colleagues. A friend of mine from work — we'll call her Martha — came to the first session, and ran into me at work the next day.

"I enjoyed playing a lot!" she noted exuberantly. "We should do it again."

She looked down at her shoelaces.

"Well. . . apart from all those random people. Next time, I think it should just be us," she said, before proceeding to list only the names of the people she knew.

Notwithstanding my firm belief that sports should be a sacrosanct forum where all are allowed and encouraged to play together, I was disappointed. There's no doubt that Martha simply believed she would have more fun if she personally knew all of the players. But I believe that she may have found that she got more out of it if she opened herself up to the colleagues she did not know, as well. At worst, you decide you don't like their company, and you move on with life — at best, you discover a lifelong friend.

But more fundamentally, I am reminded of something a friend at my first job in Seattle once told me. Michael got engaged when he was twenty-three. He was, and remains, totally in love with his high school sweetheart of over six years. And yet, he told me that the fundamental key to his content rested in one firm belief.

"At the end of the day, you have to be happy by yourself. Someone can make you feel better and amplify that feeling by a hundred, but if you can't derive happiness from being alone, then nobody can provide it for you."

I firmly believe that.

There is great power in traveling alone, even if just once. If you find that you are comfortable by yourself, you will be able to fully grasp that you are in a good place. More likely than not, you will make new friends, experience some fascinating adventures that you would have missed out on, and still be able to return to the people you love back home at the end of it.

Put yourself out there.

Chapter 11:
Do the right thing

December 17-18, 2013
Trans-Siberian Railway → Tyumen, Russia

I looked out the double-barred windows as the frozen landscape zoomed by.

The further away from St. Petersburg we proceeded, the more barren the horizon became. Few flora and fauna have the stamina to flourish, let alone survive a Russian winter. And yet, there was a strange beauty in the still nothingness — the crisp whiteness — of the outside world.

Russia is one of the most sparsely populated countries on the planet, with fewer than ten people per square kilometer. Bangladesh, by contrast, packs over one thousand people per square kilometer, making it greater than one hundred times more crowded. In reality, Russia is even less densely populated than the numbers seem, heavily skewed upwards by the urban metropolises of Moscow and St. Petersburg.

When the Chelyabinsk meteor hit the country in 2013, it killed no one despite packing a punch thirty-three times more powerful than that of the US atomic bomb which decimated Hiroshima. In fact, approximately one hundred years earlier, an even bigger meteor exploded near the Tunguska River in Siberia. It was the largest impact event in modern recorded history — and still, not a single soul perished.

Suffice to say, the world got lucky when those meteors chose Russia. If the same projectiles had landed in Tokyo, perchance, millions would have been lost.

And yet even this description cannot do justice to the sheer desolation that is Russia. One can go hours on the train — hundreds of miles — without seeing the remotest signs of life.

Nonetheless, here we were — sharing a train with hundreds of Russians chugging eastward towards their unlikely homes, curious as to the story behind these American young adults who appeared rather painfully out of place.

I walked up and down the cabins, chary at first of drawing too much attention to myself. In Moscow and St. Petersburg, I was certainly unique — but by no means one of a kind. But the more we moved east, the more my skin tone made me a bonafide celebrity — albeit, perhaps not the most popular one.

One of the benefits of ignorance of the local language is a corresponding blissful obliviousness to the content of what those around you think of you. Nevertheless, it was difficult to lay low when our fellow travelers openly gaped and pointed, whispering clandestine thoughts to their neighbors as I strolled by perfunctorily. For the moment though, none had the courage nor the inclination to approach me — an arrangement that suited me just fine.

Exploring the train was a process awash with small, unexpected delights.

For instance, I was fascinated by the bathrooms. The flush mechanism opened the literal bottom of the toilet bowl, exposing it to the underlying ground and depositing one's excrement directly onto the tracks beneath. The freezing cold was such that holding down the handle for an extended period of time would cause the inside of the train bathroom to fill extensively with snow and sleet from the outside. Like a mischievous child, I often amused myself by turning the bathroom into a winter wonderland for the unassuming passenger waiting outside to be the next in line for the loo.

Moreover, each section of the train contained a different, cutely designed dining area. I enjoyed people-watching, observing strange foods being eaten, and watching passengers descend into extreme states of inebriation over long periods sitting alone at the bar. When you are trapped in one place for so long, you have no choice but to find ways to entertain yourself.

Our first destination on the train was the city of Tyumen. It was located two thousand miles away from our starting point in St. Petersburg and about sixteen hundred miles east of Moscow. The town was established in 1586 as the first Russian outpost in Siberia, contains about half a million people nowadays, and presently serves as the de facto headquarters for the Russian oil and gas industry — close to the Kazakh border.

Of course, these facts were only revealed to us ex post facto. At the time, we had simply picked a random city on the map and decided it would be a fine place to visit.

Nothing less, nothing more.

It would take two full days of transit to arrive, so we dug in our heels for the journey at hand. I spent hours lounging on the bed above our mysterious Russian compatriot listening to music on my iPod Shuffle while Avi and Jeremy lay across from me. But as night fell, I had completely drained the device of battery.

"Shit," I said. "Does anyone have a charger? I forgot to bring mine."

Jeremy and Avi shook their heads.

No music for the rest of the trip. I was bummed out, but had no one to blame but myself. Just as I had begun to accept this unsavory reality, the man below me raised an outstretched arm with a Shuffle charger and adapter in it. He unclenched his fist and asked, "You need?"

"*Da!*" I exclaimed. "*Spasibo!*"

Yes! Thank you!

And just like that, we became friends with Slava — the first of many subsequent strangers who would show us great kindness and warmth on the trip.

Slava was a young man, in his mid-twenties, who hailed from the city of Perm. His area served as a major industrial center near the Ural Mountains located on the shores of the Kama River. The young man had recently graduated from a state university in the city with a prestigious engineering degree in tow. He had traveled to St. Petersburg to take on some client work and was returning back home to continue pursuing his vocation.

It soon became rather evident that Slava — an unassuming and diminutive pale man with a soft face and slim frame — had an intellect to match his boundless generosity. A voracious learner, he soon began demanding that we teach him English numbers, mastering the entire set up to one million within the course of an hour. He then asked us myriad questions, a clear front to improve his mastery of the language.

Where were we from? What were we up to? And, most importantly — *why Tyumen?*

We didn't have a satisfactory answer for that one.

After some banter, Slava pointed to our chess board and asked if he could play.

"Are you very good?" I asked.

"No. I am a beginner," he fibbed. "Let's just play for fun, though."

Confidently, I seated myself at the board. Fewer than three minutes later, my king had been vanquished.

"You're a hustler!" I joked.

"Again," he requested.

Slightly demoralized, but taking solace in the fact that it couldn't get much worse, I rose up for the challenge once more. On my second move, I played a knight out in front of my pawn — a classic opening for me.

"Take it back," Slava demanded, a look of disgust etched upon his face.

"What?"

I was perplexed.

"Take it back," he repeated. "Trust!"

"Let's just play it out, Slava," I replied, bemusedly.

Irritated, Slava proceeded to pantomime the following eight hypothetical moves that would proceed my catastrophic turn — demonstrating, beyond a shadow of doubt, that a loss was imminent if I played the move I had insisted upon.

"Jesus," I thought. "Am I playing Slava or Garry Kasparov?"

Sheepishly, I pulled the piece back. But it was of no use. Resistance, as they say, was futile.

Within ten minutes I had been defeated again — and so too, would Avi and Jeremy subsequently fall. After he had knocked off the three of us, we decided the only recourse was to take him down a notch, and we had just the antidote to do so — alcohol.

We pulled out a couple of forty-ounce bottles of Gold Mine beer — a substance so poor it garnered a three-percent rating on BeerAdvocate.com[19] — and imbibed with our new friend before passing out for the night.

Smiles were shared and laughs were had. This was what we had come to Russia for.

---

19   Every frat daddy's favorite resource, this website ranks beers on a scale of 1 to 100.

Lesson

In elementary school, we often had class competitions — the speech contest, the math contest, the geography bee, and the like. While I would prepare rather assiduously for the respective events, I often approached the actual competition days quite loosely. I had put in the effort, and the chips were bound to fall as they may. Most of these competitions are now a distant memory, but one event in particular left an indelible mark upon me.

It was the sixth-grade spelling bee.

The top three representatives from grades five through eight were set to go head to head. The winner of the competition would go on to represent our region in the qualifiers for the Scripps Howard National Spelling Bee, so the stakes were somewhat high. Nonetheless, I remained my jocose self, cracking jokes and exchanging pleasantries with the other eleven finalists.

That is, until a gangly eighth-grader approached me and asked for my name shortly before we were set to take the stage.

"Hey, I'm Vijay," I replied good-naturedly. "What about you?"

We'll call him Akhil.

"So Vijay, how long have you been preparing for the competition?" he inquired, rather nosily.

"Well, I've done some studying, but nothing too crazy," I responded coyly, intentionally choosing not to flip the question back at him.

Nonetheless, Akhil did not require an invitation to show off.

"I've studied a lot," he said. "Many hours each day. I've watched all the previous Spelling Bees, gone through the Oxford English Dictionary several times, and studied all the roots and etymologies extensively."

"That's awesome, man" I said. "I'm sure you will do great. Best of luck out there."

I won't lie — I was intimidated.

Akhil seemed like he had put in a lot more work than me, and I looked at him with some level of trepidation. I still wanted to win, but I felt that my chances had taken a distinct blow even before the competition had begun. As the late Prodigy[20] would say, I was "shook."

Akhil was the first contestant in the single elimination contest. The early rounds started with easier words, and the list got progressively more difficult as the tournament progressed.

As he stepped up to the mic, the moderator announced, "Akhil, this is your first word."

He nodded confidently.

"Nozzle."

A quizzical look passed over Akhil's visage.

"Nozzle. . ." he repeated.

His fists clenched, and he fidgeted in place.

"Nozzle," he uttered once more, this time less assuredly than the last. The seeming bravado of his prior interaction with me had, in an instant, evaporated.

"Can you. . . use it in a sentence, please?" he stammered meekly.

"Tom went to the gas station and pumped fuel through the nozzle," stated the overseer, monotonously.

"Nozzle."

Akhil's face remained puzzled. Then it turned blank.

He was in trouble.

"Nozzle," he repeated nervously. "N-O-S-L-E. Nozzle."

Ding.

"That is incorrect," said the announcer.

Muffled, somewhat sympathetic applause accompanied Akhil's swift exit stage right. And, in that moment, I learned something extremely valuable.

Intelligence is not something to be spoken of. It is something to be demonstrated. That's why the smartest people in life tend not to be the be the loudest advocates of their own brilliance — but rather, they tend to be the most unassuming.

At face value, Slava did not appear to be the sharpest tool in the shed. But within the course of a few hours, his own brilliance

---

20   One half of 'the infamous' Mobb Deep, a hip-hop duo out of New York City.

naturally revealed itself to the group. Not because he banged on a table and shouted about his intellect, but because it emanated through his actions, unable to remain obscured from plain sight.

Throughout life, we encounter multiple intellectual challenges — from job interviews, to exams, to debates. Though I am far from brilliant, I always make it a point to try to follow Slava's lead. If someone asks how the event went, I almost exclusively respond, "It went OK. Neither great nor awful, but I did my best."

There's nothing more off-putting than the person who constantly brags about their own brilliance, only to find out later that the results did not pan out as they purported. There is no point in puffing yourself up, because reality will reflect the truth — one way or the other — and words cannot obfuscate that.

The same general principle applies not only for intelligence, but for virtually any desirable trait that you can think of. The person that trumpets themselves on social media as a progressive and generous soul is likely not as close to the vision he portrays as the person who eschews posting about it in lieu of actually *doing*.

I am reminded of one of my favorite anecdotes of all time.

It pertains to the legendary Dean Smith, head college basketball coach at the University of North Carolina in Chapel Hill. When Coach Smith was an assistant coach at the school in the 1950s, segregation was still a de facto way of life in the American South. However, Coach Smith — a white man — had struck up a friendly relationship with a black pastor in the area. The two of them made dinner plans to meet up at a restaurant in Chapel Hill one night.

The pastor was fearful. He mentioned to Coach Smith that being seen with an African-American in the restaurant could get him into trouble, and potentially even fired. Coach Smith, however, paid no mind. The two sat and enjoyed their meal together without incident — and nothing more was ever said of the encounter for several decades.

That night marked the beginning of desegregation in the city of Chapel Hill.

When interviewed about this event much later in his life, a reporter asked what inspired the coach to dine with the pastor. Dean Smith responded angrily.

"Who told you about that story?"

The reporter, taken aback by the ostensibly cantankerous nature of Coach Smith's response, told him that he had heard the story from the pastor himself. Coach Smith grunted, and brusquely retorted, "he shouldn't have told you that."

The reporter was befuddled.

Why, he asked, would Coach Smith want to hide such a beautiful story from the world? It was, after all, quite perplexing that he did not want to let people know the truth about what had really transpired on that fateful night in Chapel Hill.

Coach Smith looked at the reporter, took a deep breath, and responded.

"We should never be proud of doing the right thing," he stated. "We should just do the right thing."

Be the person you want to be, and don't worry about the recognition. If you are deserving, there is no doubt that it will show.

Chapter 12:
Laughing at you or with you?

December 18-19, 2013
Trans-Siberian Railway → Tyumen, Russia

We woke up the following morning at the crack of dawn — which, for Russia in the middle of winter, meant that it was already almost noon.

Slava had previously roused and was hurriedly packing up his belongings. His stop was imminently approaching, and he would be disembarking shortly.

It was a bittersweet moment. Just like that, our first real Russian acquaintance was on his way. We exchanged email information, said our farewells, and embraced as the train ground slowly to a temporary halt.

"Promise to stay in touch!" he said with a wry smile as he hopped off the train.

"*Da svidahnia!*" we replied in unison.

Goodbye!

While we were sad to see our new friend depart, we were eager to continue our journey. We were getting closer to Tyumen, the site that would mark our first official excursion onto Siberian soil. For the time being, though, we settled into our now slightly more capacious compartment and passed the time amicably between chatter and chess.

We tried to bask in the tranquility of the barren, sparse landscape that passed us by. But even with the door to our cabin closed shut, we found that our halcyon space was continually disturbed by persistently loud noises from the neighboring compartment. While we had simply tuned them out while Slava was around, we found the distractions increasingly difficult to ignore in his absence.

There was no doubt that this rambunctious behavior was at least in part induced by alcohol. Indeed, a teetotaler would find the journey on the Trans-Siberian to be unpalatable, if not overtly odious.

Abstinent we were not — in fact, Avi, Jeremy, and I were far from it. But I don't believe any of us were truly prepared for the remarkable level of abject drunkenness we would encounter on the train. On the Trans-Siberian — nay, in Russia as a whole — alcohol is just as ubiquitous as water flowing from a tap.

Anyone who has been on a plane is familiar with the pouches of water that come with a meal, replete with an easy-to-use horizontal peel-off top. In Russia, vodka is routinely served in these same pre-packaged containers — as available, and almost as cheap, as plain spring water itself.

It is a quotidian sight to the average Russian, but jarring to most anyone else — and certainly to a group of American twenty-somethings. You will encounter people downing pouches of vodka in a rote, cursory, and almost mechanical manner at most any time of the day.

Breakfast? With vodka. Lunch? With vodka. Skipping a meal? Acceptable.

But god forbid if you skimp on the vodka.

It was a way of life, and it showed. Not simply in the auditory sense of the cacophony of drunken chaos. Nor only in the visual sense of the quasi-comical but simultaneously concerning imbalance of the permanently tottering boozehound.

But also in the statistics themselves.

As of 2015, the World Health Organization defined Russian life expectancy at sixty-four years for males and seventy-seven years for females. While women are naturally expected to live longer than men, the rest of the massive disparity between male and female longevity can be explained almost entirely by their respective rates of alcohol consumption.

Russian men imbibe copious amounts of alcohol. By some accounts, they drink more than the men of any other country in the world.[21] Subsequently, they live shorter lives than their female

---

21   I hear the Irish and Korean contingent may want to have a word with me, though.

compatriots — a function both of cumulative liver damage and of enhanced propensity to make unwise, inebriated decisions resulting in immediate fatality.

And so this was the subtext for the situation that played out presently with our disruptive train neighbors. It was an annoyance, but an expected one — and one that we had willingly signed up for by making the trip. I walked out of our compartment to investigate the scene next door, strolling by casually and sneaking a furtive glance inside.

It was precisely as expected.

The table inside the compartment was stocked with bottles of alcohol. Eight young Russian men lounged together, all between the ages of eighteen and twenty-four. They were dressed in army fatigues or shirtless, existed in various stages of intoxication, and took myriad hits to the face — pulling alcohol straight from the bottle. In addition to their piercing shrieks, bouts of hysterical laughter, and bellicose mannerisms, one of the boys had connected a loud speaker to his iPod and was blasting Russian hip hop over the top of their conversation.

I returned to our home base, chuckled, and described the scene to Avi and Jeremy.

"Honestly," Jeremy said, "it sounds pretty fun. We should join them."

We laughed, opened up some alarmingly molded bread for a quick lunch, and loosened up a bit ourselves. But just as we began to settle in, there was a loud rapping on our compartment door. We paused, hoping that perhaps it was just a drunken mistake.

No luck.

Seconds later, the ruckus persisted. And the uproarious laughter emanating from the compartment next door made it clear precisely what was happening. One of the young men had been dared by his friends to come spy on their exotic neighbors next door, and this boy — replete with liquid courage — had no intention of flunking the task.

"Here we go. . ." I thought, rising up to get the door.

Just as I stood up to acknowledge our uninvited guest, the door flung open and a shirtless young man welcomed himself in. His gaze glazed over Jeremy rather quickly, and his eyes fixated upon me.

"*Privet!*" he shrieked.

Hello!

He stumbled over, plopped down on the seat beside me, and extended his lanky right arm around my shoulder. The boy leaned in a little bit too closely and started talking briskly in my ear — an encounter made all the more uncomfortable not only by my lack of comprehension of his Russian and his vigorous touch, but also by the fact that he suffered from a severe case of alcohol-induced halitosis.

Shielding my nose from the odious smell, I chuckled to Avi and Jeremy.

"I don't know what the hell is going on."

The proclamation triggered an instant shift in the boy's mannerisms.

"English!" he proclaimed. "*Americanskiy!*"

American.

His tone was rather truculent, but his face appeared soft. It seemed fitting to respond with an appropriate level of caution.

"Yes. . ."

"Where exactly. . . you from?" he probed further.

"California," I answered.

The response unfailingly elicited awe in the eyes of Russians — and, additionally, in the eyes of all foreigners in general. Indeed, I had come to bask in the glory of declaring that I was a Californian. The sense of adoration and adulation that people instantly had for the place — and, by transitive association, for me — never ceased to flatter me.

"You must know all the movie stars," was a common response — unbeknownst to the Russian that Los Angeles was six hours away from San Francisco by car, and that the sprawling city was large enough that I could plausibly live my entire life there and never once run into a singular A-list actress.

A similar response tended to accompany Avi's standard answer to the origins question — New York. Though Avi was from New Jersey, he had come to claim New York as his standard place of living over the years for two reasons. First, nobody knew what New Jersey was. But second, and more importantly, New York was the only place that could draw a reaction even remotely similar to the instant fawning that always came with my proclamation of Californian residence.

And that left poor Jeremy.

His response of "Tennessee" necessarily resulted in one of two binary responses. Either the questioner's face would become totally blank — entirely clueless as to the whereabouts of this mysterious white man. Or the inquirer would respond, rather tentatively, "*Jack Daniels?*" A third-rate whiskey brand was the only thing putting this man's place of birth on the map.

And in this situation, it played out largely to script. My response of California instantly intrigued the young man, who took it as a slightly awkward, but entirely non-threatening invitation to scoot even closer to me than he already was.

"I have friend from California! He go to. . . Sacro? Sacarato?"

"Sacramento," I corrected him.

"He go, Sacramento! He love California!" the boy slurred, excitedly.

I reached out to connect with the outstretched arm of the crapulent young army boy.

High-five.

The boy then exchanged similarly overexcited commentary with Avi about New York, name-dropping several friends of his friends that had either lived in or studied in the state. Jeremy, by virtue of his provenance — and, likely, his pale skin tone — was almost summarily ignored.

Starting to grow sufficiently comfortable with our guest, I began inquiring as to his backstory. What was his background? Where was he going? Where did he hail from? Was he, as his attire indicated, a member of the Russian military — or was he just sartorially inclined to make us believe so?

"You are correct," the adolescent responded. "Me and my friends. . . we the Space Army!" he uttered in broken English.

He did his darnedest to stifle back laughter.

"You know space army?" he asked excitedly.

I was afraid I did not.[22]

Either the boy had had too much to drink, or he was attempting to poke fun at us. I began to suspect the latter when the lad pulled out his phone to take some point-blank pictures of me and made a couple of half-hearted attempts to pat my afro — all of which I rebuffed,

---

[22] As it turns out, the youth was likely referring to A.F. Mozhaysky Military Space Academy, an aerospace training school in St. Petersburg.

respectfully. Regardless, the experience was turning from cautiously friendly to increasingly discomfiting.

After a few more minutes of general boorishness, he demanded, somewhat incoherently, that we come over and meet his friends.

"I think we're OK," Jeremy replied. "It was nice to meet you."

"No, you must meet friends!" he insisted. "You — wait here!"

He bolted out of the compartment. Within a minute, seven additional curious and inebriated young men had streamed into our pod, examining me as if I were some sort of endangered or unfamiliar species.

At this point, the conversation morphed into something entirely unintelligible. Incomprehensible questions were shouted, thumping music was played, numerous arms were placed around coldly uninviting shoulders, and much alcohol was consumed — contributing to an atmosphere of utmost debauchery.

When the boys finally got tired of our muted responses to them — a couple of hours later — they headed back to their compartment. But not before capturing sufficient photo and video content of me.

Involuntarily, of course.

To this day, I am convinced that hours of video exist somewhere on the Russian internet of the drunken army boys in our cabin filming me — though I have yet to track it down. Perhaps I am a local celebrity.

The thought is, on one hand, strangely nostalgic. On the other hand, it is plainly terrifying.

Our interaction with the so-called "Space Army" was indescribably bizarre, but I must admit I was happy it had concluded.

I welcomed meeting all sorts of strangers on the train — particularly ones our age. And, moreover, this group was not openly aggressive nor overtly hostile towards us in any discernible manner. If anything, their crime was that of being overly friendly.

But there was one thing that I just couldn't make out. And it kind of bothered me.

Were they laughing with us or laughing at us?

Lesson

My father Jai came to America in 1977 to pursue a graduate degree in computer engineering.

Four years later, he took on his first job at the IBM Research Center in San Jose. He remained at the company for thirty years — a feat that I find nearly unfathomable, having myself switched companies twice in the first five years of my career. Along the way, he claimed over sixty patents, become one of fewer than two hundred living IBM fellows, and received various accolades for his visionary work in the field of computer storage.

It would have made sense for me to follow in my Dad's footsteps. But I, for one, was never particularly interested in computer engineering.

My childhood is colored by memories of after-school visits to my dad's workplace. Apart from hanging out in his office and admiring the awards he had collected, I would often exchange awkward pleasantries with his technically brilliant, but sometimes socially inept colleagues. One question would unfailingly present itself.

Namely, what did I want to do when I grew up?

"Do you want to be a computer engineer like your Dad?" his coworkers would ask eagerly.

"I'm not sure yet," I would respond. "But I really like journalism and politics."

My Dad's colleagues would generally shake their heads disparagingly at the response. They would offer uninvited avuncular advice in a manner that always seemed, at least to me, stingingly sanctimonious.

"You should be an engineer," they offered. "Then you can solve real problems. After all, it has worked out quite well for your Dad. Isn't that right, Jai?"

It was an easy set up. They would gaze longingly at my Dad, hoping — expecting, rather — to receive his prompt affirmation.

But he always refused to offer it.

"Vijay can do whatever he pleases," he would reply. "He is doing very well in school and he has plenty of time to decide for himself what he wishes to pursue."

An awkward silence would ensue. And then, eventually, the topic of conversation would shift.

My Dad's advice left an indelible mark on me at a time when I was highly impressionable. It encouraged me to pursue a T-shaped worldview,[23] one characterized by a broad pursuit of interdisciplinary passions — from writing to politics, to math, to science. Most importantly, it inculcated in myself the belief that I could do anything.

That I was my own person.

As I progressed through school and eventually into college, I coped with a minor inferiority crisis. I still did not know precisely what I wanted to major in, but concentrations like Political Science and English had piqued my interest. Meanwhile, virtually all of my friends were streaming confidently into Engineering and Computer Science programs — the STEM majors. I would often talk to them about my passions, but I felt as if I would summarily get shut down.

The problem — that my interests were not sufficiently *technical*. This, they surmised, meant that "anyone could do them." And if anyone could write or debate politics, then why should I waste my time studying something so boringly universal when I could join the ranks of the technical myself and be able to garnish this superior skill set to 'change the world'?

It was a lie so compelling and so pernicious that I eventually found myself buying into the myth. The humanities were for the weak. And I wanted to be part of the strong.

I ended up graduating from Duke with a double major in Statistics and Economics. While not *super technical*, the former, at least, gave me the street cred that I was looking for in terms of intellectual respect.

Though I do not regret my decision to major in Stats — a degree that I find incredibly useful to this day and that has sparked several divergent passions of my own — I regret the thought process that led me into pursuing it. Essentially, I am disappointed that I was railroaded into it by the social stigma surrounding me.

---

23   The vertical spike of the 'T' represents depth in a particular area of expertise while the horizontal top represents breadth across different disciplines.

The truth is, there is nothing special about "technical."

Technical is a myth designed to elevate those who pursue STEM degrees to an imaginary pedestal above the rest of the world — the ostensible plebeians who pursue the arts and the humanities.

Sure, "anyone" can write.

But "anyone" can code too. "Anyone" can become a statistician. And, yes, "anyone" can be a physicist.

Not everyone can be great, however.

Not everyone can be a great writer. Nor can they be a great coder. A great statistician. Or a great physicist.

That is what requires practice, dedication, and commitment to the craft. And that is what we should all pursue — greatness within and beyond our disciplines.

Not just the discipline itself.

Recently, I was driving down from Seattle to my new job in San Francisco. My Dad had come up to road trip with me. We made a pit stop the first night in Ashland — a beautiful town in Southern Oregon. Over a beer, I pressed my Dad for reflections on life. I was twenty-three, and I felt as if I still didn't quite know what I wanted to do.

I exhibited all the outward characteristics of success. I had been promoted, I owned a key piece of the business for a service used by one out of every fourteen people on the planet, and, by comparison to what he had accomplished at the same age, I was making my father look like a relative pauper.

And yet I still wasn't sure if I felt successful — or content.

I asked him why, as a prominent and successful Silicon Valley engineer, he had not prompted me to follow his lead as an engineer. Maybe then, I could have felt a sense of purpose with my life — and been on a pre-ordained path destined for nepotistic success.

He paused, before thoughtfully responding.

"I raised you and your sister to be good people, above all else," he said.

"If I did my job in cultivating you into smart, respectful, and moral individuals, then I knew that everything else would fall into place. It is not my responsibility to influence your vocation. I felt confident that if I had done my part as a parent, then you two would go on to make us proud in whatever you chose to do.

He looked at me wistfully. "And, thus far, you have."

I related how much I appreciated my Dad's approach. It meant the world. But, I asked, how could I gauge my own success?

My Dad proceeded to elocute around the concept of a "stretch goal." Everyone needs to set one, he said. It should serve as your personal North Star — the invisible hand accompanying your life.

"So what was your stretch goal?" I asked.

"I wanted to win the Nobel Prize," he said, without the remotest hint of sarcasm.

And I believed him.

The conversation with my Dad inspired me to do two things — follow my own passions with unabashed and boundless energy, and set my own stretch goals. At the end of the day, we are the sole arbiters of our own lives. Our dreams should never be beholden to the skepticism of others.

We all have the capacity to change the world. We should never let the dubiety of others detract us from pursuing work that is meaningful to us.

Relentlessly pursue your passions, and brush off the ignorant skepticism of others. They can laugh with you, but they can never laugh at you.

Chapter 13:
Try > Succeed

December 19, 2013
Tyumen, Russia

The nearly forty-eight continuous hours we had spent on the train without respite began to take its toll on the group. A hot shower — or, at the very least, a change of compartment to escape the raucous atmosphere of our Space Army neighbors — would have been both welcome and salubrious. But such an outcome was a sheer impossibility.

The Trans-Siberian does not offer the luxury of choice.

Jeremy, who less than three days prior had been effusively singing the praises of train travel, had presently launched into a jeremiad against the inefficacy of this interminably long method of transport. The three of us were, to say the least, becoming irritable.

Temporary discomfort, however, was to be expected — an inevitability of the journey we had undertaken. We were venturing deep into the heart of Siberia in the dead of winter.

And I wouldn't have it any other way.

In an effort to raise morale, Avi and I offered to make a quick pit stop at the next scheduled train stop to scrounge for alimentation. Our supplies were running short, and we still had one night to conquer before landfall in Tyumen.

As per our previously agreed upon rules, at least one person had to remain on the train at all times in case of emergency. This individual would be responsible for carrying all of our luggage through to Ulan Bator in the event that the train were to depart without some of us. On this occasion, Jeremy was due for the task.

Avi and I hopped off the locomotive in the middle of a pounding snowstorm — myself ill-attired in a heavy parka and some baggy Duke basketball shorts — and made our way towards the various neighborhood mom and pop stores that lined the surrounding block. These shop owners practiced what, in my estimation, had to be one of the most remunerative professions in Russia, if not the world.

Selling food to starved and disoriented passengers stumbling off the Trans-Siberian? Perhaps the easiest sales pitch of all time.

We had fifteen minutes before the train would depart, so we entered the nearest store and browsed the aisles for snacks. In preparation for this excursion, Avi had spent the past twenty-four hours on the train memorizing the Russian expressions for various useful phrases such as "where is the cheese?" and "how much does a loaf of bread cost?" He somewhat abashedly approached the woman at the check-out counter and began to ask — in broken Russian with horrific pronunciation to match — for assistance.

Yet rather than being upset with his inability to properly communicate, the woman responded with a ready smile. She spoke little English, but managed to point us in the direction of the bread and cheese.

I must admit that I followed none of their conversation. I, for one, had not been a diligent student of Russian on the train. But even to the layman, it was evident that Avi's work ethic had paid off. He was able to converse with the intrigued shop owner — describing where we were from, where we were headed, and what he thought of Russia so far.

When it came time to check out, Avi handed the shop owner a wad of cash. She summarily refused it, instead opting to lump in some extra generous portions of bread and various types of different Russian cheeses that we had not selected.

Avi and I shook our heads, indicating that there must be some sort of misunderstanding. But the woman insisted, and pointed towards the door.

This, she signaled, was not a mistake.

She was giving us the food for free. It was a goodwill gesture — a grand Siberian welcome.

We wanted to refuse the woman's kindness, but she was persistent — and we had a train to catch. All we could muster was a genuine "*spasibo!*"

Thank you!

The incredible kindness of the woman touched us, and we ripped open and devoured our new treats rapaciously as we ambled leisurely back towards the train tracks.

There was, however, a problem brewing on the horizon.

When we had arrived at the station, our train was the only one on the tracks. Troublingly, there were now three sets of trains — two that had just recently arrived — and neither Avi nor I remembered which set of tracks our vehicle was on. As we crossed the overpass to get back to the station, we heard a loud bell ring, signifying the imminent departure of one of the vessels.

"Shit!" I thought. "Are we really going to miss out on the Trans-Siberian over a loaf of bread?"

A train started to move, and my heart sank into my throat as I sprinted towards the platform, stumbling occasionally in the snow.

"Tyumen?" Avi and I shouted to nobody in particular, but towards everybody in general.

Our pleas were ignored until an elderly gentleman calmly sitting on a bench behind us tapped me on the shoulder and pointed towards a particular runway. Avi and I ran over to the correct train and hopped on just as the engine began to rev.

When we spotted Jeremy staring concernedly out of the window, we knew we had made it.

"Jesus," he said. "I thought the next time I'd see you guys would be in Mongolia."

Jeremy, too, had been tricked into thinking the train would leave without us. He was looking outside when the train on the adjacent track began moving, fooling him into believing that it was actually his carriage that was in motion.

Finally relaxed now that we were back in the compartment, we shared some warm bread and cheese and subsequently passed out for the night.

Crisis averted. Sustenance attained.

Lesson

Michael Jordan is universally recognized as the greatest basketball player who ever lived. The players that immediately followed — try as they might — could never escape the enormous penumbral shadow that he cast over the game.

Though a surefire Hall of Famer and one of the greatest ten NBA players ever, even Kobe Bryant would never shake the burden of living up to the overwhelming standard of being "the next MJ." The issue irked him so much that he changed his jersey number from 8 to 24 halfway through his illustrious career — one above Jordan's iconic 23. Though Kobe has never publicly copped to the reason for the "random" numeral swap, one doesn't have to read too far between the lines to acknowledge the reality.

He wanted to one-up MJ — if not in reality, then at least symbolically.

In today's era, the mere insinuation that a player could be compared to Jordan is viewed in many basketball circles as an utter abomination.[24] When Jordan's ex-teammate Scottie Pippen had the temerity to suggest that LeBron James could be greater than His Airness, he found himself at the center of a maelstrom of controversy from NBA players and pundits past and present. Under intense scrutiny, Pippen was forced to renege his renegade viewpoint just a few days later.

For a player to garner such ubiquitous accolades, he must be near the top of his profession from a skills standpoint. And indeed, Jordan was one of the most skilled players to ever lace up on the hardwood.

But that alone is not enough.

After all, when we think about MJ's signature moments — the career-defining games — we often fixate on one.

"The Flu Game."

---

[24] As sportscaster Stephen A. Smith would say, "blasphemy!"

In a 1997 Game 5 Finals matchup against the Utah Jazz, Jordan powered through a bout of food poisoning and viral infections to score thirty-eight points. In the process, he led his Chicago Bulls to victory in a game that most thought he wouldn't even be able to suit up for.

From a numbers standpoint? MJ's statline was quotidian. After all, the man *averaged* more than thirty-seven points a game for an entire season in 1986.

So why does this performance — a seemingly pedestrian one by MJ's lofty G.O.A.T. standards — resonate so meaningfully with us?

For one simple reason.

He tried.

In life, there is only one thing that we value more than being the best. It's making the effort. So when Avi walked into that store outside the station and asked for bread and cheese in the most abhorrent, discordant, and butchered Russian ever heard east of Moscow, the shop owner, perversely, reacted with great aplomb.

She loved it.

She appreciated that he made the effort. She respected, most crucially, that he tried. And she demonstrated it by bestowing upon us gifts of bread and cheese.

One of the qualities that I value most about my girlfriend is her willingness to try. Though we are different in myriad ways, she is always open to new things — whether they be ideas or perspectives — and willing to give anything a shot.

This, to me, is the fundamental tenet of all good relationships — the commitment of a partner to try, even when it is tough. The worst thing we can do in the world is to rest on our laurels and close our minds and bodies to new ideas, opportunities, and learnings.

We may not be the most qualified for the job. We may not be the most prepared. We may not be the most informed. And we may not even be remotely close to ready.

But we should always be ready to try.

Chapter 14: To belong

December 19, 2013
Tyumen, Russia

As we arose in the wee hours of the subsequent morning, our vessel was slowly rolling to a stop at the train station in Tyumen. We were ready to set foot in our first official Siberian destination.

A veritable rite of passage.

We excitedly packed our belongings and disembarked.

Tyumen was like a scene out of a postcard. It was a winter wonderland, entirely ensconced in snow and ice with several more inches continuing to fall into the early morning.

As we exited the station and wandered towards the city center with no ultimate destination in mind, I started to make a habit of saying "*privet!*" to the gaping bystanders I encountered on the street.

Hello!

The greeting generally elicited a somewhat bemused, somewhat astonished non-response. It appeared that — minus the alcohol induced temerity — the reaction that people displayed towards me in Tyumen was not remarkably different from the reaction that the Space Army boys had demonstrated on the train.

A dark-skinned face in these parts was, evidently, not something to be seen everyday.

Though our itinerary was mostly open, there was one agenda item in Tyumen that could not be missed. The *TripAdvisor* page for the city lists perhaps a total of four sights to see in the city. But there is one that stands alone — transcendent, on a wintry pedestal.

It is the "Lover's Bridge."

The modern interpretation of the bridge was conceived in 1987, serving as a pedestrian walkway over the Tura River which lay dormant, frozen in ice, below. The monument is to Tyumen what the Golden Gate Bridge is to San Francisco, or the Empire State Building to New York. It is the centerpiece of the town.

And the three of us — all ironically single at the time — needed to see it.

As we approached from afar, the brilliant silver cables of the bridge came into sight, juxtaposing crisply against the snow-white backdrop over the frozen waterway beneath. As with many other similarly romantic bridges in the world, couples commemorate their visits by placing locks on its railings.

It felt strikingly out of place — boundless and eternal proclamations of unconditional love, expressed in, quite literally, the harshest of locales.

But there was something stirringly tranquil about seeing these myriad expressions of beauty and commitment emanating from the depths of soulless Siberia — a place that sometimes feels as if any emotion outside of melancholy is anathema to life itself.

Behind the Lover's Bridge, we spotted a grandiose Russian Orthodox church with two golden onion domes reminiscent of the classic style of St. Basil's in Moscow and The Church of Spilled Blood in St. Petersburg. It being a Sunday morning, the service was fully in session.

While none of us fit the appropriate demographic, we decided to enter and observe the ceremony — mostly out of curiosity, but, I am ashamed to admit, partly out of a desire to escape the harsh cold. Nonetheless, we were treated with the utmost respect by the congregation. We proceeded to participate in the religious programming for the next quarter of an hour — an experience that, while not altogether life-changing, did leave a robustly positive impression upon me.

The three of us then proceeded to *Cafe 37*, a small modern restaurant, to grab a bite and relax. Most importantly, we were looking for a place to use the restroom without the threat of a frozen bottom. This spot — while otherwise mostly forgettable — fit the bill.

Rested and relieved, we rolled back onto the streets of Tyumen and continued our unlikely, utterly random journey.

Over the course of the next six hours, we passed the time in all sorts of unlikely ways. We entered a university hall and sat in on an indecipherable advanced chemistry lecture in Russian, went to a gun store and fired deadly Kalashnikovs, visited an odd monument called Siberian Cats Park lined with marble statues of leopards — one that we actually expected to house live animals, fostering subsequent disappointment turned into amusement — and traversed through a random strip mall trying on furry Russian hats, buying strange groceries, and investigating the black market for technology items along the way.

Of course, our journey through the city exposed a striking range of different reactions.

The university students were the most curious, approaching boldly and asking for the details of our trip. The pedestrians at the park were mostly bemused, captivated by the spectacle of Avi attempting to scale a marble tiger in his impractical *Adidas Sambas*. And the shopkeepers couldn't help but smile and laugh as Avi and Jeremy tried on their various fur hats and snapped photos of one another.

It couldn't help but feel like, in many ways, an out-of-body experience — if only for its abject strangeness.

And it was true. On surface, we didn't belong here.

Honestly, I struggled to put together an explanation for what business we had being in Tyumen. It certainly wasn't a tourist destination for any Russian, let alone for an American from California.

But nobody seemed to mind. And that, for what it's worth, made us feel a tad bit more comfortable.

The overall experience was so absurd that we decided to concoct a moniker for it.

#Tyumen.

No other explanation was needed for whatever else may follow.

Lesson

There is a pernicious myth that holds so many of us back from unlocking our full potential in this world. It is familiar, and it is altogether devastating.

Specifically, it is the idea that "you don't belong."

And while we may inveigh against the mystic spell that this damned lie binds upon our society, we also acknowledge that it is so inexplicably difficult to break precisely because at its very core it is something that is embedded deeply into our individual DNA.

Human beings are innately tribalistic.

We seek comfort in clans.

In clubs. In groups. In silos. In those that look, act, and talk like us.

In communities that ostensibly bind us together, but in actuality rip us so terrifyingly far apart.

Even the ideas we take for granted — take, for instance, those of nationality or party affiliation — are mere figments of this insidious social construct. The idea that I should need some higher-level permission — a passport or a visa — to visit a brother or sister living in a different latitude or longitude is plainly preposterous if one thinks about it long enough. And yet it is merely accepted as an ineluctable inevitability of life.

But that is the sad truth. Like begets like. And it explains so much of what we hate to admit about the dark underbelly of our society.

For instance, that only 6 percent of spots at "top-tier" universities in the United States are held by African-American students despite their demographic for that age group comprising 15 percent of the population.

Or that women hold only 20 percent of Engineering degrees in the United States despite comprising 50 percent of the population.

Or that fewer than ten women — in sum total — took the Advanced Placement Computer Science Test in eight separate states in America in 2015.

There are, without a doubt, a number of factors that contribute to these statistics. This isn't a research paper, and I don't intend to pettifog over the minutiae of what those various components are.

But one factor, indubitably, is this.

Some of us are told, throughout life, that "we belong." And others of us are told, in unmistakable terms, to "get out." Far too often, males are the beneficiaries of the former message. And females and minorities are at the receiving end of the latter.

As a male, I've largely been incubated against the latter message. I have been told that I am destined for greatness, interminably reminded of my unlimited potential, and forced to believe nothing less than that I, equipped with unparalleled genius, am the sole arbiter of my own future success.

And, quite frankly, it worked. I believed, and I "achieved."

But here in Russia lay a small reminder for me of what many women and minorities have to deal with every day in America and around the world.

What it is like to feel out of place. What it is like to feel left behind. What it is like to live with the "soft bigotry of low expectations."[25]

And in my case, nobody was even demonstrably unwelcoming. It was simply my skewed perception of the situation at hand that caused my own inherent discomfort.

But that is the thing — even if we keep telling women and minorities that they belong, they may not always feel it.

#Tyumen, in addition to being incredibly fun and memorable, was also a deep learning experience.

I recognized that I need to overcome my own insecurities to reject the notion that "I don't belong." And I also realized that it is the responsibility of those around me to help make me believe it, too — to foster a more welcoming and inclusive environment for all.

So just as the Russians who smiled and laughed with me in Tyumen did to make me feel more at ease, I hope we are all able to reciprocate to those around us who may have yet to break the spell — to overcome the illusion.

You don't belong if you still believe in the myth of "you don't belong."

---

25   Notwithstanding the political baggage attached to this *Bushism*, I do believe there is something to the concept of low expectations holding people down. Let's expect greatness.

Chapter 15:
Embracing curiosity

December 19-20, 2013
Trans-Siberian Railway → Irkutsk, Russia

We spent a grand total of eighteen hours on the ground in Tyumen, spanning just the length of time from our early morning arrival to our late night departure.

Perhaps it should have felt rushed. But to me?

This was perfect.

At my essence, I am and always have been an ambler, drifter, and perambulator — the caricature of the restless soul. Indeed, at my first internship at Microsoft, I was once lightly chided for my propensity to "roam the concourse unprofessionally", a trait that earned me the humorous nickname, "the nomad."

So I was content to be moving, as Jay-Z would say, on to the next one. It behooved my peripatetic nature just fine.

And, after all, we were on a tight schedule.

Mongolian Christmas was just five days away, and we still had one more Siberian city to explore. From Moscow to Tyumen, we had covered two thousand one hundred kilometers thus far. Next up was Irkutsk, home to Baikal — the largest and oldest freshwater lake in the world.

Only 3,049 kilometers to go.

We headed to the station late at night obscured under the cover of darkness. This time, we took great pains to arrive a full hour early so as to avoid the oft-repeated trauma of nearly missing the train. Thankfully, such precautions proved extraneous on this night.

Almost a week into our trip, we had become relative experts in the field of Siberian transport. The three of us had attained a certain level of comfort reading our Cyrillic train tickets, figuring out the appropriate platforms, and identifying the proper compartments. So, at 22:00 hours sharp, we promptly and readily embarked on the next leg of our journey.

As Tyumen lay in the middle of the Trans-Siberian railway, the train was nearly at capacity when we boarded — filled to the brim with weary travelers from the West. And unlike before, the conditions actually resembled those of a third-class carriage — tight and compact, yet just capacious enough that one wouldn't feel the need to complain.

For the first time, the group was separated, albeit only by a few compartments.

I was seated across from a pale septuagenarian with sunken eyelids and a circular face, wearing a nightgown and traveling solo. Jeremy was one compartment in front of me, attempting to camouflage into the ragtag group of Russian travelers surrounding him. Avi perched a couple compartments behind, operating stealthily to avoid drawing attention.

As I sat down, I took a moment to conduct my frequent personal safety check: wallet, passport, & phone. In this case, the latter was missing — I had been robbed a few days prior to the trip — but the former two were still, much to my delight, fully intact. I pulled out my passport and took a moment to casually flip through its various pages.

Today, I carry two valid and interchangeable US passports, an arcane possibility known only to the savviest of travelers. The first contains several extra pages. The original form was incapable of holding the contents of the visas and stamps required for all the places I have traveled to. The second passport serves as a sort of contingency plan — one that I have had to utilize on the rare occasion that, for instance, one passport lays dormant at a foreign embassy awaiting visa approval while a concomitant voyage abroad necessitates the use of the other.

Looking back at the stamps in my passport never fails to foster a deluge of pleasant memories —and on this occasion, it was no different. However, I had not bargained for the genuine curiosity the act of flipping would elicit from my newfound neighbor, the elderly woman across the way.

She leaned in and extended her worn right hand towards me, wrinkled palm facing upwards. No words were exchanged, but I knew the gesture well enough. I placed the document in her hand

and watched her sullen eyes awaken as she leisurely thumbed through the passport herself.

"I," she pointed at herself, "only here." She motioned towards the window.

This woman had never left Siberia, let alone been outside of Russia. At twenty years old, I had covered more ground in the past week than she had in seventy years of life. Instantly, I was overwhelmed by two powerful emotions.

Primarily, gratitude. The fortune that had blessed me with the possibility to make this trip was one that I knew better than to take for granted. But, secondarily, and more pervasively, I was struck by pangs of guilt.

Why was I blessed with this privilege that she had been denied? And why had I been so flippant as to gloss through my passport in front of her?

Thankfully, jealousy — that most rotten of human emotions — was nowhere to be found in this remarkable old woman. She simply pointed at the stamps and asked questions. And less through my words — curse my lack of Russian — but more through my wild gesticulations, I feel as if I may have been able to transmit to her some of my favorite memories from my travels abroad.

She simply watched and smiled.

A connection without comprehension. Something I had come to appreciate more and more throughout my time in Siberia.

Moments later, we were jolted awake by a kerfuffle in the compartment ahead of us. Curious as to the source of the altercation, I jumped out of my seat and looked on. What I witnessed were the slurred imprecations of a visibly drunk, shirtless, and tattooed man extending a pointed finger in Jeremy's direction to complement his hostile exhortations. My fellow traveler merely looked on blankly — a mixture of confusion and bemusement etched upon his bearded face.

Jeremy is never one to back away from a situation. So while I did not like where this particular incident was headed, I was calm knowing that he was at the helm.

Shortly, I found that I was not the only one who had leapt to my friend's defense. Indeed, my elderly neighbor had walked over from our compartment to give the irritant a piece of her mind. Though she appeared diminutive next to the towering man, her words cut him down to size instantly. She verbally castigated him for bothering Jeremy, refusing to let up until he meekly resigned back to his own cabin without another whimper.

Though I could have figured as much merely by watching the situation play out, another English speaker on the train later filled me in on precisely what had just transpired. The drunkard who confronted Jeremy had gone on a xenophobic rant against him — angered by his presence on the train, his colored companions, and his inability to speak Russian. The older woman had rallied to our defense, along with several others on the train.

It was a "what would you do?" moment straight out of John Quiñones' playbook.[26] And our elderly savior had passed the test with flying colors.

This, I came to understand, was Siberia at its heart.

Yes, there were minor occasions of nativism or racism. But they were so wholly overshadowed by the genuine goodness of the people who showed unabashed curiosity towards our stories and who backed it up with boundless displays of goodwill towards us.

Shortly before calling it a night, I headed over to the restroom. Doing so required a brisk walk through many compartments, exposing me to a great variety of travelers. There were many single males, likely returning home for the holidays from work on the mines. There were a few families, huddled together trying to avoid the pestilence of the drunken youths.

And then, there were the army boys.

I was prepared for them — my experience with the Space Army had alerted me to their ubiquity — but, nonetheless, I always found the walk through their compartments to be somewhat unsettling. Despite the late hour, all of the young men, ages eighteen to twenty-four, were fully awake and dressed in their army fatigues. The sight of me — a young brown man in baggy basketball shorts and a monochromatic *Nike* hoodie — created a palpable sense of excitement that I could not dispel despite my best efforts to covertly tip-toe through the carriage.

---

26   Quiñones hosts the popular television show *What Would You Do* where paid actors enact uncomfortable or seemingly dangerous situations while hidden cameras record whether or not unknowing bystanders jump in to help out appropriately or ignore the situation at hand.

Heads around me popped up, shoulders were tapped, and fingers were pointed. I suddenly came to a fascinating realization.

I was the first person of color that these boys had ever seen.

And they sure were not bashful about it. So for the first time in my life, I was being cat-called.

For them, the intrigue lay in getting my attention — and I had to hand it to the army boys for their creativity.

As I was about a third of the way through the carriage, a young man called out "*Salaam Aleykum.*" I don't speak Arabic, so I kept on walking.

Another third of the way through, a young boy shouted out, "*Negr!*" This is the Russian word for black — but I'm not black, either. So while I considered it a strange breach of decorum to refer to a stranger solely by their perceived skin tone, I continued awkwardly trudging forward.

As I approached the end of the hallway and reached out my hand towards the bathroom door, a final desperate plea reached my ears that I will never forget.

The young man exclaimed, "*Wu Tang Clan!*"

This time, I couldn't help myself. I turned around and burst out laughing. The rest of the compartment broke out into raucous laughter as well, and myriad high-fives were exchanged.

The ice was finally broken. A veritable Siberian Christmas miracle.

Connection without comprehension had struck again.

Lesson

Riding on the Trans-Siberian *can* be an uncomfortable experience. After all, as an American — and a colored one at that — you are instantly the object of unwarranted attention.

I often joke that my experience on the train will be the closest run-in with celebrity status I'll ever have in my life. And for a reclusive personality like myself, that is not always easy.

But I am convinced that riding the Trans-Siberian doesn't *have* to be uncomfortable. As with most things in life, it is simply what you make of it.

One of the key things I learned early on the train was that it is imperative to embrace curiosity. And that requires having thick skin.

The "Wu-Tang" experience I described above is just one of many similar exchanges that were experienced on the train, not all of which are fit for print.

Curious stares followed me around. Incomprehensible foreign words emanated towards me. Unfamiliar fingers tapped my shoulders. Unsolicited camera snaps flashed. And, I concede, it was altogether unsettling.

That is — until I learned to embrace that curiosity.

Of course, these incidents — which took place every fifteen minutes over the course of two weeks — left me feeling distressed at first. But what I began to realize is that these gazes, questions, and interactions were not meant to offend or to intimidate. Rather, they were goodwill efforts by ordinary Russians to learn more about me and my culture.

Occasionally, the questions would border on the absurd — but only when viewed from my narrow American vantage point.

One oft-repeated inquiry was the following — "why are you traveling together?"

The question was generally posited with a particular emphasis on why Jeremy — a white male — was traveling with myself and Avi — both people of color.

And at first, this offended me. It struck me as racist to even pose such a question. But I soon understood that it was far from that.

It was legitimate and genuine curiosity.

For these folks who had only seen Siberia, the concept of interracial friendship was something that they could not wrap their minds around. Indeed, I understood that the query they expressed to me was not the one they had actually intended to formulate.

You see, the real question on their minds was not *why* — but *how*.

How are you guys traveling together?

To which we posited a very simple explanation — we were roommates at a university in America, each with our own back story and origin, and we decided to make this trip together.

Upon recognizing this basic premise, not once did a stranger react with anger or disgust. They were, almost universally, genuinely pleased. It was a concept of friendship that they had never heard of, but one that they could certainly get behind.

And, moreover — they wanted to be friends with us, too.

This epiphany hit home in many ways.

As an Indian male, one question folks often direct at me is, "do you speak Indian?" It's a seemingly innocuous question, but one that used to irk me to no end.

Of course not, I would respond. There is no such language as Indian.

And, indeed, if one were interested, they could read up on the country and realize that there are over twenty official languages in India along with hundreds of other dialects. The one my family happens to speak is Malayalam.

The smugness of my response would generally leave the questioner feeling downtrodden. Meanwhile, I felt a pang of superiority — minor schadenfreude, if you will — for calling someone out on their perceived ignorance.

But today when I get this same question, my demeanor is vastly changed. Rather than bristle, I embrace the inquiry. I welcome it. And I smile. Because it means that someone out there is genuinely interested in learning more about me and my culture.

And she is not afraid to ask.

The opinion I am espousing here is far from popular in today's society — I may even go so far as to call it robustly unpopular. But I stand by it.

So let me introduce a narrowly tailored caveat. This does not mean that it is a good idea for people to walk up to others of different ethnic backgrounds and ask, "so, what are you?"

But it does mean that if a person makes a genuine, good faith attempt to learn more about you, it is your obligation to answer with respect rather than a petulant hissy-fit.

Think about it this way.

The person that asked me if I speak Indian may very well be viewed as ignorant. But why should she be expected to know about my culture if she didn't grow up in it? Why should I be angry that she is making an effort to get to know me better? And when was the last time I bothered to ask her about her family history?

When we get questions that we feel are silly, we have a choice to make that is binary in nature — to react with hate, disgust, and negativity, or to react with appreciation and harness the positive energy of mutual understanding.

So try and embrace curiosity, even when it feels strange.

Most of the time, it will help us understand one another better and feel more comfortable around each other — something that the world dearly needs right now.

Chapter 16:
On multi-dimensionality

December 20-21, 2013
Trans-Siberian Railway → Irkutsk, Russia

When I awoke the next morning, I was startled by the figure of a portly, bearded Russian man standing over my cot. He appeared to be in his mid-twenties and his stance, while not overtly threatening, aroused a heightened sense of early-morning chariness.

But it was not so much his appearance that worried me as it was his clothes.

The young man was attired entirely in black. Emblazoned across the front of his shirt was an all-white swastika, crisply juxtaposing against the dark black background. I knew perfectly well that this was not the reverse-facing swastika of Nazi notoriety, but nonetheless, primordial thinking kicked in.

A larger white man standing over me in my compartment on a train in Siberia, in my estimation, spelled nothing but trouble. So when the stranger began to talk at me in forceful and harsh Russian, jabbing his finger aggressively in my direction, it did little to allay my concerns.

My initial response was instinctive non-reaction. A coy shrugging of the shoulders.

It took a couple of minutes, but the man finally got the hint. His words were falling upon deaf ears, and he finally departed the compartment. I breathed a quick sigh of relief and ventured out to brush my teeth and freshen up.

Much to my chagrin, I exited the lavatory only to find the same man barreling down the hallway in my direction. I ducked into my cabin and closed the door.

Seconds later, there were three loud knocks. I took a deep breath and opened up.

The man walked in and took a seat beside me. Behind him trailed an additional uninvited guest. She was a young blonde woman, probably around my age, and she seated herself on the other side of me. The swastika-bearing boy gestured towards the doe-eyed girl who looked towards me with great uncertainty.

She fidgeted, clearly uncomfortable, and mumbled, "you... speak English?"

"Yes," I nodded.

The boy looked at us wide-eyed and expectant, as the girl continued.

"Okay," she stammered. "I do not know him, but he said there was a foreigner on board. He wants to ask you some questions. I will translate?" she offered, intonating in such a manner as to obfuscate whether she was offering a statement or asking a question.

I looked back at the boy and reverted to her.

"Sure," I agreed, cautiously.

The girl and the guy rapidly exchanged words in Russian as she filled him in on what we had just discussed. Then, the questioning began.

The man was immensely curious, and I was on the hot seat. But his curiosity was good-natured, and his questions were relatively tame.

Where was I from? What was I doing here? Since I was from California, had I met all the famous celebrities yet? Are the houses and cars really as luxurious in the States as they appear on the television? What did I think of Obama? Of Russia?

The girl — we'll call her Nastia — patiently and sweetly translated the dialogue between myself and the man, Ivan, for some hours.

After some time, I got in on the questioning as well.

What did Ivan and Nastia think of America? Of Putin? Of me? And what were *they* doing on the train?

As it turned out, Nastia was returning to her parents house after a brief visit to her maternal grandparents before the Christmas holiday. Ivan had just received leave from university and was on his way back home as well. And, for what it's worth, neither of them thought particularly highly of Putin.

As the minutes turned to hours, that initial tension I had felt rapidly evaporated. These were new friends. And thanks to Nastia, our trusted translator, we had crossed a previously unreached boundary — connection *with* comprehension.

Pure, unadulterated dialogue.

And yet, I felt foolish.

That scintilla of fear I had felt when the black-laden Ivan approached me for the first time had once again been rendered superfluous. That sense of discomfort that I had been working so hard to deracinate — while severely repressed — had still managed to persist and poke its ugly head again.

Judging a book by its cover, as it turns out, is almost always a mistake.

Nastia and Ivan had shown the wherewithal not to do so by approaching me — an alien — of their own volition. From this point forward, I made a mental pledge to do the same.

After much mingling, Nastia asked, "So. . . he wants to know why you are traveling alone?"

"Oh," I responded. "I totally forgot! I am here with two friends. Let me go find them."

I roused Avi and Jeremy from their respective states of somnolence and introduced them to the new crew. We shared some stale instant noodles and chatted for a few more hours before the seemingly tireless Nastia finally demonstrated weakness by requesting a brief respite back to her carriage — but not before we made plans to link back up later.

After whittling away a couple more hours watching the frigid landscape pass us by, we met up with the two of them again in the early evening. Nastia pulled out some scrumptious braised cabbage piroshki that her grandmother had baked for her and shared it generously with the group.

Avi and I gobbled up the food voraciously, our already gangly bodies withering away without real sustenance on the train — much to Ivan and Nastia's bemusement. Jeremy, while also ravenous, exercised considerable restraint in showing it. We knew we embarrassed him, and we reveled in it.

Though alcoholism knows no limits in Russia, visible drunkenness becomes nearly ubiquitous in the evening hours. It was on display that night, as multiple elderly men stumbled by in a daze.

They leered at me and Avi, strangers in their land, and lusted at Nastia — a young, beautiful girl. One man, clearly old enough to be her grandfather, even brushed her kneecap on the way by, feigning total ignorance as he lumbered through.

These sights made us all uncomfortable and angry. I asked Nastia, "Are you okay?"

"Yes," she responded recalcitrantly. "They are just drunk. These things are common here."

It seemed like a sad reality, I responded. Surely things did not have to be this way.

"True," Nastia replied. "But it is changing. The younger people are not like this. They are much more accepting. They want things to be. . ."

She paused, searching for the right word.

"Different."

Avi passed out a round of beers, and we cheered to that.

A time-tested reality. Dr. King's moral arc bending towards justice.

As the evening progressed, we shared more food, drinks, and laughs. Ivan, via Nastia's translation, suggested a quick type of cultural exchange — to share our favorite movies, music, and books. I passed over some recommendations on Rich Homie Quan's newest mixtape and Ivan and Nastia suggested the Russian girl group Serebro. Neither group, I can confidently report, was better off for having participated in the exercise.

Later in the night, an elderly drunk man came over, and, unlike the other transients who had wandered through over the course of the preceding hour, insisted on staying in the compartment with us. He attempted to communicate, but his words were so slurred that even Nastia could not translate their meaning.

Nonetheless, the man's spirit was genuine. He sang traditional Russian songs over and over again, patting my shoulder and cajoling me to repeat in chorus. On the rare occasion that I made the effort, he got up and clapped joyfully, bellowing the song ever and ever louder.

After a couple of beers, I felt a desperate urge to use the restroom. Because the train was stopped at a station, the doors were locked — standard procedure for the voyage. I returned to the compartment and related this situation to Nastia. The old man insisted on knowing what we had discussed, so she repeated it back to him.

Instantly, the man rocketed straight out of the compartment, beckoned me to follow, and flagged down an official. After witnessing his quick and harsh conversation with the conductor, I found the door to the bathroom unlocked for me. The least I could do was burst out into song — and we both danced and laughed in the hallway.

Right as we were about to call it a night, Nastia took a look at her phone and her radiant smile transformed into a deep frown.

"Everything okay, Nastia?" I asked.

"Yes, it's fine," she muttered, downcast eyes at odds with her statement. "It's just... those people get away with everything."

"What people?" I asked, devoid entirely of context.

Nastia proceeded to outline how a terrorist attack had been committed. The perpetrator had been identified — a young man from the North Caucasus.[27] I probed a bit more.

"Well, surely they're not all bad people," I offered.

"But it is *always* them," she retorted. "We are not allowed to say it, but this is the truth. And it is simply not fair."

"Have you ever met someone from there?" I inquired.

She looked back at me.

"No."

"Had you ever met someone that looked like me before today?"

She shook her head again.

"Am I who you thought I would be?"

She studied me closely.

"No," she said, with a pang of shame in her voice. "You are not at all who I thought you would be."

I looked at her. Her gaze dropped and a sadness enveloped her eyes.

"I see your point," she said. "You are right. It's just hard sometimes."

I gave her a hug of understanding, and we called it a night.

---

[27]   A region in Russia that has been dogged by low-level insurgency in recent years.

Lesson

I have had this discussion with many of the best and brightest minds I know. Some agree and many more do not.

That is okay. Disagreement is welcome, as long as it presents itself constructively.

But allow me to lay out the case for you. I contend that it is possible to be fearful of different people — whether it be by religion, race, or creed — without being a bigot.

Islamophobia, in my estimation, is not inherently racist — though it very well could be. Rather, it more often than not reflects pure ignorance.

Nothing more, nothing less.

Nastia, for instance, is not a racist. She suffered from the pestilence of ignorance fostered by a lack of connection with the people she fears. She admitted as much when she talked to me.

Our conversation made her realize that colored people did not have to live down to the burden of low expectations she had envisaged for them. If she did not grock it entirely in that moment, at some point she will realize that the same applies to her countrymen from the North Caucasus as well.

I hope our conversation helped expedite that process — but the one thing that will make the change happen most quickly will be befriending or meeting someone from there first.

Sadly, though, we human beings are so quick to judgment — to categorize others. We paint broad strokes precisely because they are simple. In doing so, we ignore the reality that most of us are proverbial icebergs, with layers of character to peel away — some revealing the good, others revealing the nasty.

And such is the case even with many liberals — a group with which I associate that ostensibly prides itself on acceptance and understanding. Yet we summarily dismiss others who do not subscribe to our "echo chamber" viewpoints. We promulgate the spread of public shaming and actively espouse a dangerous call-out culture.

To many liberals, a conservative must necessarily be stupid, racist, or any other superlative embodiment of evil one can ascribe to another. We cannot fathom the possibility that they may indeed be good people who depend on certain policies — perhaps, for instance, coal-mining job opportunities — to get by.

And of course, by treating those folks as social pariahs, we engage in the least effective method of swaying them to join our ranks.

Having one "bad" view does not make someone a bad person, nor does it mean that we should ostracize them. Conversely, it means that we should engage them respectfully to try and get them to come to reach the same conclusions that we believe so strongly in.

It is true — some folks are immovable. And some are evil.

But many more are not.

It is easy to feel despondent when you subscribe to the simple point of view. But approaching the world through a new lens — one in which it is possible for someone to do or to believe something we disagree fundamentally with, but to still be a good person — is the best possible way to get by.

And it is not mere sophistry, either. It is the truth.

I think back to my best friend's mother, a caring and respectful woman, who once stated that she was afraid of Mexicans at the gas station; or to my high school English teacher, an inspiring and giving person, who once revealed that he was fearful of groups of brown people that looked like me at the airport; or to Mark Cuban, a successful entrepreneur, who once publicly revealed his insecurities about approaching hooded black folks at night despite owning a basketball team that is almost entirely black.

A prior me would jump to shame all three of them.

Not today.

While I still firmly believe that some thoughts are better left private, I now recognize these comments for what they are. Not simply expressions of old, racist white people. Not a virulent scourge of overwhelming prejudice.

But honest vulnerabilities.

We do not live in a world of bigots. We live in a world of people who are scared.

Headlines, narratives, and soundbites influence perceptions of reality. The only way to get around this is to make connections with the people who do not look like you. That, to me, is the essence of travel — and the textbook case for diversity.

I once emailed the CEO of my previous employer, Microsoft, with the words, "I would be happier to work at a place where there are fewer people who look like me." And I damn sure meant it.

So while it may seem like we are living through an era of dark political and social change — an era where bigotry and intolerance appear to be on the rise — I rest assured knowing that most people are still fundamentally good.

In *The Story of My Experiments with Truth* Mahatma Gandhi said it best: "When I despair, I remember that all through history the way of truth and love has always won. There have been tyrants and murderers, and for a time they seem invincible, but in the end, they always fall — think of it, always."

Think about that. Always.

And so, this too shall pass.

Chapter 17:
Think like a child

December 21-22, 2013
Trans-Siberian Railway → Irkutsk, Russia

Another sun had risen and set on the Trans-Siberian, though one could be forgiven for questioning the adage.

Indeed, the further we moved east, the more we found ourselves enveloped by abject darkness. In some of these parts, the sun rose at noon and set fewer than three hours later. Relentless snow pelted the train irrespective of the hour.

I could not help but wonder how dramatically changed this environment would look a mere six months later, in the dead of summer. But for now, the important thing was that we keep chugging forward.

Four days until Mongolian Christmas.

Nastia and Ivan had disembarked at stops along the way — Novosibirsk and Krasnoyarsk, to be exact. We were sad to see our new friends leave, but deeply thankful for our interactions.

They had opened our eyes up to new perspectives — and so, we hoped, had we unto them. And though our transmogrification into real Siberians was not yet complete, we felt at least a little more confident that we were on our way.

With our rations of instant noodles and bread beginning to run low and our insides starting to feel a bit bilious, Avi and I determined that it was time to give the dreaded dining cart a shot. We headed over to the compartment, chess board and cereal box in tow, and — after much pantomiming — were able to obtain a copy of the menu with pictures.

Luckily, there is one common language in the world — the language of numbers. Unluckily, the prices were too damn high for these two cheap college students.

We harrumphed, returned the menu, and relegated ourselves to a far seat in the dining room where we could play chess, absorb the frigid views outside, and pick away glumly at our stale cereal box. The plan went smoothly for about ten minutes until a server walked over to our table and asked us, presumably, to order something.

We motioned, I wagging an index finger and Avi shaking his head, hoping she would catch our respective drifts. After about a minute of this painful exercise, a nearby passenger in his mid-forties with a grizzled beard, crumpled argyle sweater, and slightly too-tight khakis interjected in English on our behalf.

"She says that if you do not order anything, you cannot eat at that table," he translated. "You are welcome to sit and play, but you cannot consume your own food."

A fair request. We thanked the gentleman, nodded our comprehension, and sent the waitress on her way, impressive high heels clicking away.

Naturally, our reaction was to do what any college student would have done in that scenario. We simply hid the box of cereal underneath the table and proceeded to sneak in some clandestine bites between chess moves. This worked perfectly until, in a fit of chess-induced rage, I accidentally kicked over the box of cereal — spilling corn flakes all over the compartment.

And then came the familiar *click-clack* of the lady in the heels.

She was headed over once more. I braced myself for the scolding that was to come.

The woman walked up to the table, looked down at the mess, wrinkled her nose in disdain, and then, inexplicably, plopped down a large stack of *blini* — Russian pancakes.

Avi and I looked at each other in shock.

I went through the full gamut of emotions. First came the euphoria of potentially free food. Then, the lost-in-translation moment of despair when you realize you may be on the hook to pay for something you didn't order.

But the woman in the heels allayed my concerns totally when she simply pointed across to the gentleman in the dress shirt and walked away. It dawned on us — he had paid for our meal.

And so we instinctively pushed the plate away.

"Please," we pleaded. "You should not pay for us."

But he insisted.

"I was a college student once," the man — we'll call him Dmitri — stated. "I remember what it was like to try and get by, meal to meal."

We nodded, resonating with his words.

"When I saw you two eating your cereal under the table, I was reminded of myself."

I was struck by the profundity of what the man related. Here were two young colored men interacting with a middle-aged white man in Siberia. And Dmitri had pushed through the external facade so nonchalantly to establish a real connection with us.

We were touched.

Dmitri proceeded to ask us a bit more about our trip and our travels. He mentioned that he had a five-year-old son who was fascinated by the world, and he hoped that one day his boy would have the privilege to travel as well. I pulled out some various bank notes that I had cobbled together in my travels through the world and handed them to Dmitri so his son could start a collection of his own.

We thanked each other and headed our separate ways. When we returned to our compartment, we found Jeremy surrounded by a mass of Russian boys, between the ages of ten and twelve.

"What's going on?" we asked.

"They are part of a traveling youth hockey team," Jeremy responded. "They were curious about us, and now they want to hang out."

The boys — twelve in total — were an absolute pleasure to be with.

They asked us all sorts of questions, wanted to hear what was on our iPods, hustled us into helping them with their English homework, and demanded to follow us on Instagram. And they, in turn, emboldened all sorts of other people to come and talk to us — everyone from young female students who were too scared to approach before, to older male professionals who had been too judgmental to do so.

It was the boys' first interaction with foreigners, something that in Siberia is restricted almost entirely to the realm of YouTube — and they were enamored.

And we, in turn, loved the kids.

While many groups on the trip had made us feel welcome, this was the first group to truly make us feel accepted. Because for all the myriad people and groups we met on the journey, this was the only one that failed to mention the color of my skin or to ask why we were here.

Rather, they inquired about two separate things altogether — where we were from, and how we enjoyed Russia.

We hung out in a cramped compartment the entire day and into the early hours of the next morning when we had to depart, arriving at our next destination — Irkutsk. As we exited, the boys shed some tears as they watched us leave from the windows. Walking towards the podium of the station in Irkutsk, we were halted by a collective shriek.

We turned around to witness an avalanche of youths running towards us. They had rushed off the train — risking its imminent departure — to hug us goodbye one last time before we left.

For all of the memories made on the Trans-Siberian, this moment was undoubtedly the highlight.

Alas, such moments are stunningly transient. But perhaps that is what makes the memories so special.

It was time to get our boots dirty in Irkutsk.

Lesson

My overall experience in Siberia and with Siberians is a rosy one. People treated me, largely, with respect and curiosity. I had an incredible time and met some truly phenomenal people.

But I would be remiss if I did not acknowledge the negative aspects as well. At times in this book I have mentioned them. At other times, I have glossed over them entirely.

But if there is one group of people that always had my back — that never made me question whether I belonged — it was the children.

Children are full of boundless, positive energy. Their minds are still developing, unencumbered by the stereotypes that we lapse into as we "mature." They have not developed silly heuristics for gauging good and evil in the way that we as adults tend to do. The world exists for them, not in silos, but in its purest and fullest form.

And so it was with the youth hockey team on the train. Like the adults, they wanted to know where I was from — after all, I clearly was a foreigner. But beyond that shallow commonality lay a sharp dichotomy.

Because unlike the adults, they did not care to know *why* I was in Siberia.

Innately, those children understood what most adults do not — how alienating, even if purely innocuous and inquisitive, that question can be. Being asked why you are in a place that is not home makes you feel as if you are unwanted in that place.

As if you should not be there. As if you should pack up and leave. But the kids did not ask this.

Moreover, not once did a single child so much as bring up the glaring elephant in the room — the color of my skin. It was of zero consequence to them. These details were both obvious and superfluous.

Indeed, only one thing really mattered to the kids. That we were guests in their country — and, as our newly christened hosts, that they show us unbridled and boundless hospitality.

And therein lies a revelation. Namely, that at times it would behoove us all to take a hard look inwards and ask if there are ways that our lives would be better if we started to think more like children.

America, for all the bland aphorisms it espouses, is less a beautiful melting pot than it is a segregated wasteland. We ignore the fundamental reality that pretty aspirations are not enough if outcomes remain poor. Even our ostensibly liberal bastions — San Francisco and New York — remain mostly siloed — bogged down in the muck of identity politics.

Whites with whites. Asians with Asians. Blacks with blacks. And so on and so forth.

And it got me thinking.

At the point at which I'm more likely to befriend the random Siberian kid that I have literally nothing in common with let alone a few jumbled words of English than I am to befriend my conservative white American neighbor across the street, I should be ashamed.

We should be ashamed.

We've got to do better. We've got to start thinking like children.

Chapter 18:
Pay it forward

December 22-23, 2013
Irkutsk, Russia

It was with a sense of melancholy that we exited the train station in the dead of another frigid evening and began navigating towards *Nerpa Backpackers*, our hostel for the night. In just over forty-eight hours we would traverse the country's southern border, barely in time to ensure a Mongolian Christmas.

The end of our wild stint in Russia was rapidly sneaking up on us.

While I remain navigationally inept to this day, Avi had picked up Cyrillic well enough by this point to follow the street signs and guide us painlessly towards our nearby destination. At the door, we were greeted by Alexandra, our amiable host for the night.

"Is there anything that you need?" she asked in impressive English.

"Where is the shower?" the three of us chimed in unison.

Indeed, it had been five full nights since any of us had taken our last shower, all the way back in St. Petersburg — a distant memory at this point. Minus a brief stop in Tyumen, where we passed on booking a place to stay, there had been no opportunity to bathe.

The Trans-Siberian, for all its mystique, does not promise fine amenities.

Washing off the stench of over five thousand kilometers of travel in a spacious and scalding shower was a cathartic experience — and one that induced immediate somnolence. Exploration of Irkutsk would have to wait until the morning.

After catching some much-needed rest on a stationary bed, we arose with an immediate action plan. We were headed to Lake Baikal, an enormous antediluvian body of water whose incredible fathomage lends it the distinction of being the world's deepest lake.

We quickly synced with Alexandra who gave us the details on which bus to take and how to return. She was deeply interested upon learning that Avi and I were of Indian ancestry, noting that one of her favorite restaurants in town was a vegan Indian restaurant. Intrigued, we made plans to dine together at *Govinda's* later that night.

The ride into Lake Baikal was a fairly ordinary one, but the view it gave way to was anything but. The water was immaculately clear. What lay before us could only be described as a shimmering expanse — a halcyon time capsule serving as a peaceful respite against the turbulent backdrop of an ever-evolving history.

Sure enough, I had heard from those we met earlier on the train that Baikal would be incredible — but I assumed nonetheless that much of the hype was mere gasconade. Only upon seeing the lake with my own eyes could I believe the reality. 20 percent of the world's freshwater was contained within this singular entity, right before my eyes.

Baikal had cracked my stolid exterior. I was entranced.

The three of us roamed the shoreline for over an hour, exploring abandoned shacks, slipping and sliding across the icy coastline, and basking in the beauty of the reflective surface of the water. When we had our fill, we darted over to a nearby restaurant to catch a quick lunch on the shore and watch the waves ripple by. Then, as had been the case over and over again on this trip, we were ripped away from this gorgeous location far too soon — slaves to the rigors of a tight schedule.

We boarded a bus back into the city where we met up with Alexandra in the town square shortly after 5:00 PM. Locating her was no easy feat as the three of us lacked any phone lines for communication — but for her, presumably, finding the three swarthy foreigners was less of a daunting task.

She walked up to us with an amiable smile.

"Hungry?"

We nodded in synchrony and followed her as she proceeded to guide us through the Christmas market in the town, pointed out the notable shops and stores, and finally arrived at our destination — *Govinda's*.

It was a somewhat surreal experience — venturing so far out into the middle of nowhere trying to escape the usual comforts only to find a place of utmost familiarity. Hindu idols watching over us, we sat cross-legged on pillows around a barely elevated table and devoured reams of naan with saag paneer.

Strangely enough, Avi and I may have been the first Indians to enter the establishment. It would explain the peculiarity around why the server seemed acutely interested in whether the two of us, specifically, liked the food.

Fortunately, *Govinda's* passed with flying colors. It was surprisingly scrumptious. Satiated, content, and happy, we headed back to the hostel with Alexandra. When we arrived, her shift was up. We exchanged goodbyes, and she introduced us to our newest hostess for the night — we'll call her Tati.

Tati was a brunette with piercing blue eyes and a slender frame, who carried herself with an edgy and hip demeanor. Though her English was not quite as good as Alexandra's, we managed to connect over shared phrases or interests.

For instance, she showed us a picture of her at work at the Dairy Queen in Irkutsk — a familiar and comical sight for us. When I mentioned I was from California, she gestured with her middle finger over her ring finger, index and pinky spread far apart, and thumb folded in. Even in Siberia, they were throwing up Tupac's famous "West Coast" sign.

We also met another backpacker. The man, Garry, must have been around fifty years of age. He was currently in transit to Vladivostok, all the way on the eastern terminus of the country, closer to Japan, where he worked seasonally for half of the year.

Garry did not speak a word of English, but his charming attitude was infectious. He laughed and joked, played cards with us, and demonstrated the typical Russian flair for nonchalant chess brilliance.

At the end of the night, Tati suggested that we participate in a gift exchange — something that would let us all remember one another. We loved the idea.

I gave up my Golden State Warriors shirt — a prize whose value I could not have predicted at the time — Avi parted with a Duke Russian shirt, and Jeremy handed over a Tennessee keychain. In exchange, I received a Sochi Olympic flag, Avi scored a passport cover emblazoned with the words, "I love Irkutsk", and Jeremy obtained a menacing balaclava.

The hospitality we received in Irkutsk was a fitting end to an absurd stint in Russia. Our time was filled with various ups and downs — but most perceptibly with charity. And now, it was time to depart for Mongolia.

From Russia, with love.

Lesson

In our limited time on the Trans-Siberian, we were touched by innumerable moments of human kindness. Sadly — though, perversely inspiring in some sense — most of them cannot be properly documented in this book if only for sheer lack of space.

Indeed, this trip was the closest feeling to helplessness I could imagine in my adult life. In Siberia, I was out of my element for the weather, the language, the culture, and my appearance. I was entirely reliant on the kindness of strangers to understand the right train to board, the directions to my bed, and the contents of the food I was putting into my mouth.

At its core, my survival depended solely on trust of others.

I have always heard the term "pay it forward", but I have never seen it put in practice quite like I did in Siberia. It was evident in our everyday interactions — from the comforting smile of a stranger on the street, to the thoughtful offer of help from the local who understood that we were lost, to the translation assist from the multilingual passerby who helped us to comprehend the dinner menu.

And it was evident in those who went above and beyond — many of whom you've read about. They include, but are not limited to the strangers who purchased meals for us, offered to charge our dead iPods, provided us with free food from the shop, or gifted us with souvenirs from Russia to take back home.

Inspired by our run-ins with these benevolent strangers, I have since tried to engage in this type of gift-exchange process everywhere I go — leaving behind a trail of cultural breadcrumbs, like Hansel and Gretel, and returning with many of my own.

I am reminded of one of the most salient recurring memories of my childhood — a daily ritual my dearly departed grandmother and I used to partake in. Every summer I would travel to India to visit my grandparents in New Delhi and each evening we would take a drive around the capital city to see its various sights.

One of the unavoidable sights was stark and overwhelming poverty. When you are around it as long as we have been, you come to realize that what you see may sometimes be an illusion.

Therein lies a conundrum.

The obvious instinct, of course, is to give. But, some would argue, giving may create a perverse incentive for folks to avoid looking for work.

Nevertheless, my grandmother always gave. And when I asked her why, she said something that stuck with me forever.

"Maybe they will misuse the money," she said. "But the fact that they are on the street means that they definitely need this money more than you or me."

I think my grandmother unpacked a lot of truth in that statement.

At what point does our decision to walk past the beggar on the street become nothing more than a rationalization for our inherent greed? And even if we can rationalize not giving to beggars, can we not find a better use for our money than an incremental Friday night cocktail?

But even if you do not believe in giving to beggars — and frankly, I often struggle with the question of whether that money will be well-spent — I think my experience has taught me that there are myriad other ways to give as well.

After all, it is not just the haggard person on the street with his palms upturned towards you that requires your assistance. It could also be the perfectly healthy-looking girl who is clearly lost but too shy to ask. Or the immigrant being belittled because he cannot order properly in English from the menu.

One thing is certain — there is always someone nearby who needs a hand.

So if you weren't convinced before, I hope you are now. It pays off to pay it forward.

I'm a big believer in karma — that the things that you do in life tend to come full circle. So if you see a person in need, and you have the capacity to help — do it, and don't think twice.

Life has a funny habit of rewarding you in unexpected ways.

Chapter 19:
The golden rule of travel

December 23-24, 2013
Trans-Siberian Railway → Ulan Bator, Mongolia

Finally, our time in Russia had expired.

But I am not prone to sentimentality.

Indeed, I approached high school and college graduation ceremonies with cheer, recognizing the grand accomplishment rather than lingering on the bittersweet memories. And in this case, it was not entirely different. For while the propinquity of the train had brought us closer together as a group and left us emotionally attached to this most unlikely of countries, I knew when it was time to go — and I felt that we had attained what we set out to accomplish.

So, this was not a lugubrious occasion. Rather, it was a cause for celebration.

We had entered Siberia in the heart of Winter — and we had conquered it.

At the crack of dawn, we arose, packed up, conducted one last valuables check, and departed for the train station. Taking one final look at the hostel, I descried Tati's smiling visage waving us goodbye.

Next up, Ulan Bator.

Two days to Mongolian Christmas.

Though we had stuck exclusively to third class carriages throughout Russia, we decided to treat ourselves by upgrading to second-class for the final leg of the journey. We boarded a relatively opulent looking carriage and made our way towards the compartment. Avi and I entered and were instantly blown away.

"We got this to ourselves?" Avi asked.

"Looks like it," I responded. "Yo, Jeremy, where you at? Check this place out!"

I turned around to find Jeremy in the hallway, an impatient queue of travelers burgeoning behind him.

"What are you doing, man?" I asked. "Get your ass over here!"

"I'm trapped, man!"

The strap of Jeremy's *Osprey* backpack had caught in a door crease. To make matters worse, the hallways were so narrow that only the most svelte individuals could pass by, causing many to be stuck behind him.

"I'm coming to help," I fibbed, stifling laughter and turning around to run back to the compartment.

"Where are you going?" he shouted, flailing his arms desperately.

I pulled Avi out of the carriage and briefed him on the situation. He ran out into the corridor with his phone out and snapped a few pictures before we finally got around to emancipating Jeremy from his trap.

"You guys are assholes," he said when he finally entered the cart for the first time and plopped down his bags.

We settled down and marveled at the spacious and beautiful compartment we were in. In comparison to what we had become accustomed to, this was unmitigated luxury. Royal orange plush seats, unencumbered leg room, and a massive window to the outside world accompanied four wide beds. We pulled out a forty-ounce bottle of tasteless Siberian beer and toasted one last time to celebrate.

As the train began rolling, we heard a knock on our door. An elderly Russian woman with salt and pepper hair, dark-rimmed round glasses, and a faded purple sweater walked in and pointed at Jeremy. Her teeth — or what was left of them — were bared in smiling laughter.

Evidently, the woman had observed Jeremy struggling in the hallway and was curious as to our back story. Again, we went through the familiar rigmarole of attempting to pantomime our thoughts to her.

Nyet, we do not speak Russian. *Nyet*, we do not understand your question. *Nyet*, we are not on the wrong train.

Like most of the people we encountered on the train, this woman was uncannily unfazed by our lack of comprehension. She continued attempting to force communication, unleashing a torrent of slightly more familiar but still largely incomprehensible Russian words towards us.

Occasionally we would pick up bits and pieces here and there — but for the most part we simply grinned and nodded. This process went on for about fifteen minutes before the woman finished, patted each of us on the head summarily, and returned to her own compartment.

It was a peculiar quality of the Russians we met on this trip. They were persistent. Though it was clear we had no clue what they were saying to us, they would still glibly drone on.

And at first, I must admit that this trait annoyed me.

"Clearly," I thought, "this is a fruitless endeavor. Why can't they get the message and leave us alone?"

But by this point in the trip, I had come to truly appreciate what this old woman and so many like her were doing.

Again, she had made a connection without comprehension. I did not understand a concept or phrase, let alone a word, of what we discussed over the course of those fifteen minutes. But I was happy that the woman came.

I remember her well. She was part of what made the experience unique. And she, and others like her, were the reason that we truly felt welcome.

Our visitor's interruption was the perfect segue into watching the movie *Lost in Translation*. None of us had seen it before, but we all agreed that we would view it upon departing Russia to see just how well the film matched up with our own experience.

Upon finishing, the three of us concluded that while the movie was somewhat relatable, this trip had indeed been stranger-than-fiction. For if Bill Murray had struggled so much to adapt to life in Tokyo — a first class city with great food, significantly better weather, the companionship of Scarlett Johansson, and the benefit of riches — imagine how quickly he would have withered out in the tundra of Tyumen.

The rest of the day passed largely uneventfully until around dusk, when our train ground to a halt. A Mongolian official boarded, entered our compartment, and asked for our passports. We quickly roused, gathered our documents, and distributed them to the agent who scurried off the train. We were at the border crossing.

About half an hour later, the agent returned to the train, passports in hand.

"Which one of you is Vijay?" he asked.

I raised my hand cautiously.

A quizzical look passed over the man's face. He asked, slowly, "You went to... United Arab Emirates?"

"Yes," I responded. "Many times. Is there a problem?"

"Um," he stammered. "I guess... why?"

"Excuse me?" I asked.

"Why did you go?"

"Oh," I responded. "I have cousins there. I have gone to visit them several times."

He studied my face momentarily, as if mimicking a lie detector, and then nodded unassuredly — indicating only conditional validation. He returned our passports, and the train began moving again, ever so slowly.

"Weird," I thought.

Nevertheless, the final hurdle to Mongolian Christmas had been cleared.

We were here, with just a day to spare.

Lesson

Talking to people about my travels always elicits interesting conversation. In particular, I tend to sense a heightened enthusiasm — almost to the point of excess — when I chat with my coworkers in the tech industry.

Sure, part of it is the veneer of professionalism — the idea that we are not our true selves at work, and that we put on our best face to curry favor down the line. And frankly, this may explain a portion of the abundance of interest in my travels from work colleagues when compared to the general populace.

But I contend that the majority of it boils down to two distinct factors.

First, San Francisco — and particularly, the tech community within San Francisco — exists almost entirely inside of a bubble. We are convinced of our status at the epicenter of the universe, blissfully oblivious to the outside world — let alone the dreaded South Bay. "Building cool shit" and "solving big problems" are the mantras, and yet we walk by hundreds of homeless people each day on our various routes to work and take them all for granted as if they are mere sidenotes to the latest juice blender start-up raising millions on Sand Hill Road.

Second, there is a notorious culture of "self-improvement" that pervades San Francisco. And yet, the notion that one should pursue this course tends to come not from a place of self-reflection, but rather from a place of being told so. For instance, the SF tech community is enamored with ostensibly virtuous activities like "reading voraciously" or "traveling." Spending a couple minutes browsing Medium.com, you will find enough platitudinous book and travel recommendations to consume a lifetime. You should do these things, you are told, because they are "mind-expanding" — because they will make you a better person and a better employee.

So it is natural, I suppose, to find myself — at the nexus of these two presumably idealistic activities as both a writer and a backpacker — the subject of intense curiosity. But the truth is, reading for the sake of saying you've read and traveling for the sake of saying you've traveled are inherently pointless activities.

Reading only provides value insofar as you take away something from what you've read. If all you can say is that you've read the *Innovator's Dilemma*,[28] but you can't distill out the essence of what you took away from it, then what exactly was the point? Accordingly, I have made a habit of writing book reviews for every book I read.

Similarly, travel must carry some personal meaning to make it worth your time. It does not have to be transformative in some earthshakingly symbolic manner — perhaps it is just the memories, the people you've met, or the food you ate. But it certainly should stand for *something*.

The deeper level of fascination, however, mostly seems to stem from the particular locations to which I have traveled. Places like France and Italy make sense to my colleagues — but places like Zimbabwe, Guatemala, and Mongolia do not. Why had I chosen these off-the-beaten-path destinations?

After getting this question so many times, I formulated in my mind the answer. It is what I call the Golden Rule of Travel. And it goes like this.

Travel to a destination that is not only unique to you, but where you are unique to the destination.

Don't get me wrong — I have had an incredible time visiting Western Europe, Canada, and Mexico. But indubitably, the most rewarding travel experiences I have had — the ones that stick with me to this day, that resonate plangently, and that have left an indelible mark upon me — are the ones that have adhered exclusively to the Golden Rule.

It is not easy to find such a place in today's ever-flatter and more globalized world. Moreover, I cannot give you a list of these places, because it depends entirely upon the person. For instance, India does not meet the standard for me because I am Indian — but it may meet the standard for a white or black friend.

---

28   Clayton Christensen's seminal work inspired generations of entrepreneurs and ensured that the word 'disrupt' would be overused for time immemorial.

But for the next vacation you take, I implore you to think deeply about picking a place that meets your personal Golden Rule of Travel.

You may think it unsafe or unsound. But remember that for even the most dangerous place in the world — today that distinction belongs to San Pedro Sula, Honduras — there are hundreds of thousands of people who have lived there all their lives and been just fine. With appropriate caution, you will be, too.

Following the Golden Rule will open your eyes to new destinations you would never have imagined visiting. It will set you up for myriad run-ins with human kindness. It will allow you to experience vulnerability and to conquer it. And it will provide you with lifelong memories.

But don't take my word for it. Do it because you want to.

Self-improvement, after all, can only come from self-reflection.

Chapter 20:
Enter the portal

December 24-25, 2013
Ulan Bator, Mongolia

We pulled into the station in Ulan Bator at dawn on the morning of Christmas Eve. Avi, our resident cartographic expert, had mapped out the directions to our hostel per usual. It was set to be a forty-minute trudge from the station to *SunPath Mongolia* in freezing minus-thirty-degree-Fahrenheit weather.

It was a phase in my life that I have now come to refer to — with a mix of fondness and disdain — simply as *the Cold*. And when immersed in *the Cold*, there is frankly no option but to buck up and deal with it.

We laced up our *Timberland* bootstraps, disembarked, and set foot on the frigorific Mongolian soil. As we navigated out through the parking lot, I noticed a rotund Mongolian man in camouflage pants with an impressive goatee and heavy jowls, seemingly in pursuit. Cautiously, I nudged the group to pick up the pace.

But the hefty individual was persistent.

The next time I looked over my shoulder, the man was directly behind us. He gave me a hard slap on the shoulder, forcing me to stop in my tracks and pivot about.

"You," he said. "Come."

"No, I'm okay," I responded, turning around to continue walking.

He grabbed my shoulder again — more aggressively, this time — and pointed to a sedan behind him.

"Come now," he demanded.

"Maybe he's a driver for the hostel," Avi whispered, noting that the man appeared to be targeting us in particular.

"How could he know that it's us?" I retorted. "We didn't inform the hostel when we would be arriving or tell them what we looked like."

"I think you know how he can tell," Jeremy responded, tongue in cheek. "We don't exactly blend in."

I guess, perhaps, it was not so unreasonable to assume that the only brown people in Mongolia in the middle of winter — disoriented backpack travelers, at that — would be the ones headed to the *SunPath* hostel. So we dismissed every canonical piece of advice we had ever gotten from our parents and followed the burly Mongolian back to his vehicle.

We got in the car with a stranger.

And — contrary to the stereotypical trope you tend to hear — we survived.

To this day, I still consider it a minor miracle that the man was able to pull us out of that station. He dropped us off at the hostel shortly before 6:00 AM. We marveled at the quality service, felt appreciative for having avoided a long walk in sub-zero temperatures, and took a quick morning nap to celebrate and recuperate. When we awoke around noon, it was high time to explore and grab a bite to eat.

Our knowledge of the Mongolian language was entirely nonexistent, and whatever Russian we had picked up in Siberia now proved functionally useless. As a former satellite of the USSR, the country felt stultified by twentieth century Soviet initiatives aimed at limiting cultural and historical programs. As such, Mongolia was in the process of taking serious steps to cleanse itself of its prior Russian influence — one outcome of which was a vehement aversion to the language itself.

Consequently, when we entered our first restaurant, we were forced to pick blindly off the menu.

Fortunately, on account of beneficial currency conversion rates, Mongolia was a place where we had the luxury of guessing. Avi, Jeremy, and I each tested our luck — pointing out random characters on the pictureless menu to the bemusement of our waitress. She promptly returned with three random dishes, and I immediately recognized that mine was a winner. I devoured a steaming dish of Mongolian noodles for the equivalent of just two US dollars while imbibing some steaming hot tea.

Jeremy wasn't quite so lucky. His drink choice turned out to be a bitter type of milk. It was of no consequence, however. For an additional fifteen cents, his second drink turned out vastly improved.

We exited the restaurant contentedly and noted an immediately intangible dichotomy in the air. Whereas Russia had a staid, reserved, and tough exterior that required work to break down, Mongolia had a younger, livelier, and more welcoming aura that lay out in the open rather than beneath the veneer.

As we walked down the street, a group of college girls dressed in bomber jackets and ripped jeans giggled and pointed at us. But, in some inexplicable sense, it was so immediately clear that the group was laughing with us rather than at us. Their mirth came from a place of appreciation rather than a put down.

This latent vibrancy extended to the sartorial scene, as well. Mongolian fashion was vastly different from Russian fashion. It was flashy, colorful, ostentatious, and hip — matching its surroundings.

And in that moment, despite our fantastic voyage, the group felt pleased to be out of Russia. We felt confident, at ease, and welcome.

That night, we checked out Sukhbaatar Square — the centerpiece of downtown with a small Christmas market and a giant statue of Genghis Khan.[29] Behind it was a skyscraper with views of urban Ulan Bator. We went to the top and celebrated over a bottle of Chinggis — the national beer, named eponymously for Genghis Khan. Tributes to the Great Khan were the norm around here, as we were beginning to find out.

As the night progressed and the hour got closer to midnight — the starting point for Mongolian Christmas — we hopped to a few different bars. At one, we met a friendly waitress who was in the midst of applying to MIT, hoping to study mathematics in the United States. At another, we met a group of Korean ex-pats who had come to Ulan Bator to participate in the oil industry, but had established their own micro-community in the city — one that Avi appreciated as a vegetarian in dire need of kimchi, trapped in a country of meat eaters.

At our last bar-hopping destination, we visited an ostensible Japanese karaoke bar at the insistence of its owner. However, when we entered, we found that we were the only visitors inside. Jeremy made a quick beeline to the door to exit, only to find it locked shut.

---

29 The former leader of Mongolia spearheaded an empire that comprised the longest continuous area in recorded human history.

The Japanese man concernedly asked us why we were leaving so soon. Feeling somewhat panicked, Avi raced to a nearby window and jumped out onto the snowy patch below. Jeremy and I were about to join his lead when the man, clearly bashful about this unwarranted miscommunication, simply unlocked the door to let us out.

Upon exiting, we ribbed Avi about his escapades. He responded by shouting "push me!" Jeremy and I gladly accepted his invitation, knocking him onto the snow for the second time in as many minutes. We laughed heartily, and the spindly man forgave us promptly.

As the hour neared 11:00 PM, we meandered over towards a club that had been recommended to us so we could ring in the holiday occasion. After entering, the three of us decided to take three shots back-to-back — a group tradition on the start of a first night in any new city. Avi picked gin, I picked whiskey, and Jeremy picked tequila.

The adrenaline was rushing.

As the obvious sore thumbs in the otherwise homogenous building, we were instantly the center of attention. Hordes of revelers — from young Mongolian college students to women in Santa outfits — approached to find out more about us. One man in particular was intensely fascinated by Jeremy, asking him questions about Jack Daniels and trailing him closely throughout the night.

At one point, I entered the bathroom and found two large Mongolian men fighting. It ended with a man's ear being bitten off, à la Holyfield v. Tyson.[30] But, perhaps as a testament to the country's traditional warrior spirit, nobody seemed particularly perturbed. The folks in the restroom continued to happily urinate as the blood spilled around their feet.

As the clock approached midnight, I found Jeremy dancing alone in front of the speaker box. I corralled Avi and we got together to celebrate the culmination of an incredible trip. The dream, hatched six months ago in a bedroom in India, had finally transpired — Mongolian Christmas was here.

When the club finally shut down around 4:00 AM, a group of Mongolian college students we had befriended over the course of

---

30   Among many other things, the boxer Mike Tyson is infamous for biting off part of the ear of his opponent Evander Holyfield in a hotly contested match.

the night invited us to come back with them to continue celebrating. Jeremy and I both got in the car, before Avi pulled us back.

"Wait," he whispered. "Isn't there a chance that they rob us?"

We had already survived entering the car with a stranger once in the last twenty-four hours. Avi's warning convinced us that there was no need to push our luck. We hopped back out of the vehicle and headed home.

Maybe the story would have ended here tragically if we had gotten in the car. Or maybe it would have taken an awesome and compelling turn.

Who knows?

Regardless, Mongolian Christmas had lived up to the hype.

Lesson

As a freshman at Duke, I participated in a program called Duke Engage. The program funds service trips for students to go abroad to work on a particular problem of interest to them in a developing country. As part of the requirement for joining Duke Engage, each student must attend a compulsory orientation program.

Part of this session during my year included a keynote speech by a former Duke Engage volunteer. He entitled his speech "Drink the water." The orator got on the stage and delivered advice that must have made the Duke administrators — simply looking to limit liability — squirm in their seats.

"These people," he said, pointing derisively at the organizers, "will implore you to take a bunch of precautions. They will tell you not to drink from the tap when you are abroad."

He turned with some venom to face the pallid staffers behind him before continuing, clearly off-script.

"Don't listen to them," he declared.

"Drink the water!"

A gasp went around the room — the students murmuring excitedly while the administrators sat aghast.

The talk, of course, was meant to be an extended metaphor on the necessity of risk-taking while traveling. While I appreciated the message, I thought the wording could use some improvement. After all, drinking unboiled tap water in a developing country like India isn't really taking a risk. Rather, it is one of the most certain actions one could take — ensuring dysentery at best, if not typhoid.

While thinking up a more appropriate metaphor for what this student was trying to convey, it occurred to me that Jeremy had already developed one. In college, he often would pose a question to me.

"If a portal appeared in front of you right now, would you enter it?"

"I need more details," I would respond.

"No more information," he insisted.

"Can I at least get a guarantee that I could come back?"

Jeremy would shake his head emphatically.

"That's it. A portal has popped up. You have five seconds to decide. Do you enter or not?"

Invariably, my response was no — it seemed far too risky. And his was always yes.

But I am starting to think that Jeremy had it right all along.

The life we live consists of certain and immovable knowns. We are so paralyzed by the potential consequences of the unknown that we often give up on incredible opportunities, endlessly asking ourselves "what if?" But in the process, we tend to over-index on the negative ramifications without giving appropriate thought to the potential rewards.

Choosing not to enter the portal leaves us consigned to a life as we know it that exists within finite boundaries. Of course, entering the portal is a path fraught with danger. But it has an unfathomable upside — namely, the potential to experience something unprecedented.

One of the few regrets of my time on the Trans-Siberian was choosing not to enter the proverbial portal — the car — at the end of our last night in Ulan Bator.

Sure, there was a chance we could have been robbed. But far more likely, we would have cemented incredible friendships that we will presumably never get the opportunity to rekindle.

So the next time you are faced with a decision of unknown consequence, ditch the analysis paralysis and do as Jeremy does. Listen to your gut instincts – they are often right.

Enter the portal.

Chapter 21: Question, question, question

December 25-26, 2013
Terelj National Park, Mongolia

We awoke on Christmas for our penultimate morning in Mongolia. As we chatted with the hostel owner about what to accomplish on our last full day, she suggested heading out to Terelj National Park — a halcyon landscape on the Mongolian steppe — to spend the night.

"But where would we stay?" I asked.

The woman mentioned that she had family we could crash with who lived in a traditional Mongolian *ger* — a portable tent built for nomadic families on the steppe. It was one final act of kindness to bookend a trip filled with them. We jumped at the opportunity, and just like that, we were headed out to the barren plains.

By around midday, we had arrived at the *ger* — home to a nomadic couple with a two-year old baby girl. In broken English, they suggested a small hike up to a scenic Buddhist temple at the top of a nearby mountain.

The route to the top was, at face value, arduous — but it was designed for contemplation, relaxation, and reflection. Along the way various signs were posted, but they were not directional in nature. Rather, each sign contained a numbered Buddhist quote — a singular pearl of wisdom designed to keep your mind active on the way to the temple.

I fixated on #93, finding significance in my birth year. It read, "the sun rises on the summit of a snowcapped mountain the same way thoughts appear in a wise person's mind."

After all, insight and inspiration require extensive and wrenching contemplation. Mental acuity does not come immediately, easily, or often. Indeed, wise ideas tend to start out obscured by dark and stormy thoughts. But eventually, a mental breakthrough is reached — despite the seemingly impossible obstacles in its path.

We eventually reached the summit where we found the empty monastery — ornately carved and laden with deities, providing stunning panoramic views of the winter wonderland that was the Mongolian steppe. This was true serenity.

A Christmas Day unlike any other.

We spent a couple of hours lounging at the top while wild horses frolicked around us before the bone-chilling cold forced us to return to the *ger*, lest we fall prey to frostbite. When we headed back down the mountain, darkness had already descended on the Mongolian plains. Our host mother graciously asked what we would like to eat for dinner, pointing at various meats on the table.

"Oh, I am vegetarian," Avi said.

She shook her head.

"What? What is vegetarian?"

"Vegetarian," Avi tried again. "It means that I do not eat meat."

"Ah!" the mother nodded. "Yes, we will eat meat!"

"No, no!" Avi responded.

He pulled out his Mongolian dictionary only to find that no appropriate translation exists for the word vegetarian in the language. So he combined various words signifying "no" and "meat" together in different combinations and permutations.

But his efforts bore little fruit — there was an utter lack of comprehension.

It must have taken half an hour before Avi could successfully transmit the message. We were in a culture where the idea of consuming only vegetables was so anathema to the Mongolian experience that even the concept of such a lifestyle was simply beyond the pale. But our host graciously adapted, and we devoured a sumptuous vegetable stew for dinner.

That night, we sat around the dining table and played with the family's young daughter. The father brought out an old Windows laptop and consulted Avi's help for troubleshooting problems. The man had conflated Avi's software engineering background with an expectation of IT mastery. It was a clash of cultures that ultimately resulted in no technical fixes, but nonetheless a melding of souls.

At nighttime, temperatures dipped below minus-fifty-degrees-Fahrenheit — significantly colder than it had been in Siberia. We had to use nature's restroom out in the harsh elements, and I felt incredibly grateful to not have any stomach issues that night. After brushing my teeth and relieving myself outside, I hopped into bed in my full parka and accompanying long johns.

It was the coldest night of my life.

But I had zero regrets. When we awoke the next morning, there was only one site left on our bucket list: The Genghis Khan Equestrian Statue.

Mongolia is unique insofar as it is a mere footnote in today's global landscape, oft-overlooked in its geographic sphere of influence by other modern behemoths such as Russia, China, and Japan. Yet in historic terms, Mongolia is a powerhouse that less than one thousand years ago amassed and ruled over the largest contiguous land empire in recorded history.

At its core, Mongolia struggles with finding its footing in the new world — one in which it finds its prior dominance strictly curtailed. And this, perhaps, is why it clings so heavily to its past.

One defined almost singlehandedly by the looming figure of Genghis Khan.

Indeed, the country has an all-encompassing fascination with *Chinggis*, as he is known locally. The man is venerated, revered, exalted — the face and father of a proud nation. No matter where you go, you are unable to escape his scowling visage. The street corners are lined with statues in tribute to his rule, the currency is emblazoned with images of his face, and just about every facet of life — from beer to detergent — finds itself named eponymously after the Great Khan.

The statue, completed in 2008 with a price tag of over four million dollars, is a gargantuan one-hundred-thirty-foot stainless steel replica of the Khan on horseback facing east in the supposed direction of his ancestral birthplace. The inside of the building houses an accompanying museum with more exhibits honoring Genghis's legacy, surrounded by an accompanying ring of *gers* lining the exterior.

We ambled up to the statue, felt almost compelled to pay our respects with a genuflection, and soaked in the last few moments of our time in Mongolia. Then, we hopped in the car one last time.

Our final destination in Mongolia, appropriately enough, would be *Chinggis Khan International Airport*.

Lesson

When you are raised in a certain culture long enough, your worldview becomes imbued by certain pernicious notions that you take, unquestioningly, to be true.

As an American, for instance, you are raised to believe that the USA is the sole arbiter and defender of freedom, equality, and democracy in the world — that we have the moral ascendancy.

And yet, Americans remain blissfully oblivious to our government's daily drone strikes in the Middle East, our history of meddling in democratically elected governments from Iran to Guatemala, and our dark past that includes slavery and the original holocaust of the Native Americans. Nonetheless, we are never too quick to condemn Germany — and rightfully so — for its own grisly Holocaust.

As I flew out of *Chinggis Khan International* in Ulan Bator, I could not help but wonder how this would be any different than if I were flying out of *Adolf Hitler International* in Berlin rather than *Tegel*.

The latter was universally recognized as unacceptable. So why wasn't the former?

Both Khan and Hitler were, by the most sober modern calculations, war criminals. If Genghis Khan had lived today, he would immediately be tried in an international court and sentenced to life behind bars. But somehow, Mongolians — and the rest of the world — turn a blind eye to his barbarism. Even I, visiting his shrine outside Ulan Bator, felt a compulsion to pay respect to the man behind the statue.

There are, in my mind, two debilitating factors at play — recency bias and the curse of nationalism.

With regards to the former, it is an unfortunate characteristic of human nature that we tend to overlook events as time passes. The slaughter of Native Americans, the enslavement of African Americans, and the segregation of the twentieth century are things that we are systematically programmed to forget. The problem arises in that they still carry resounding effects to this day. By failing to acknowledge those effects, we can never make progress. Perhaps Tupac said it best when he rapped, "forgive but don't forget. . . keep your head up."

Vis-a-vis the latter, I read a quote by Sydney J. Harris the other day that perfectly encapsulated my feelings on the subject. He says that "the difference between patriotism and nationalism is that the patriot is proud of his country for what it does, and the nationalist is proud of his country no matter what it does."

I will always be a patriotic American. Being a patriot means that I have a civic duty to call out my country when it behaves in a way that does not behoove its lofty ideals.

But I will never be a nationalist.

I will never glamorize an individual that lacks decency and promotes anomie. Even if that individual supposedly "represents" me.

Even if he is the president.

The biggest takeaway is this — always question standard wisdom. Take nothing for granted. Make no assumptions.

Peter Thiel, a man with whom I vociferously disagree on most accounts, has said he finds one interview question in particular to be the most enlightening. On this specific issue, I happen to agree with him.

He asks, "what is one thing you believe to be true that most people would disagree with?"

I love this question because it forces us to reject "common sense" and to rely upon our own notion of the world.

To think for ourselves.

The moment any belief becomes incontrovertible in your life — whether it be religion, philosophy, or otherwise — is the moment you should start assailing that thought with clear, unadulterated, and unbiased reflective thought. A world unencumbered by the weight of antiquated dogma becomes nimbler, more open to debate, and more prone towards positive change.

In 2018, *Chinggis Khan International Airport* will be phased out and replaced by *Khöshig Valley Airport*. No word yet on what will happen to Chinggis beer — but progress happens one step at a time.

Chapter 22:
Do you

December 26, 2013
Ulan Bator, Mongolia → Manila, Philippines

Just like that, it was over.

The Winter Trans-Siberian experience. Mongolian Christmas. The stuff of dreams that was now, unequivocally, our shared reality.

We flew out on our separate ways — Avi to continue his journey on to South Korea, and Jeremy and myself trending downwards to the Philippines.

Since that Winter of 2013, we've all gone on to do different things.

Jeremy graduated with degrees in Psychology and German and went off to Leipzig for a year to study chimps before heading off to Uganda for a year in the jungle doing his own research on the animals. Avi finished a dual degree in Computer Science and Statistics and headed to Indiegogo as a software developer prior to joining Atrium in an attempt to disrupt the legal field. And I finished up degrees in Statistics and Economics before heading out to Seattle to work at Microsoft on Xbox and then heading back home to the Bay Area for a stint at Dropbox prior to joining Scribd as a product management lead, marrying my dual passions for books and technology.

But two common threads still bind us.

Friendship and travel.

Since that time, we have traveled to many more places together — Argentina, Chile, Peru, South Africa, and Morocco, to name a few. And while it is nice to know that the two of them will always be there when the travel itch strikes again, there is something else we intuitively ascertain deep down, even though we may not wish to admit it.

There will never be another trip like the Trans-Siberian.

Lesson

As a Duke University alumnus, I often interview prospective high school seniors seeking to gain admission to the institution. This component is just one of many others in a process that has seen admission rates slip into single digit percentages in recent years. But often times, in an uber-competitive landscape, this step can mean the difference between acceptance and rejection. In each interview, I try to learn not only about what the individual student has accomplished, but also about his or her own underlying motivations for pursuing those feats.

Judging by the former alone, I could be lulled into a false sense of optimism. It is indubitably true that each subsequent class of high school seniors is more outwardly impressive than the previous. They have racked up more awards, scooped more leadership positions, and garnered more accolades than I can remember in my time — and I'm less than a decade removed from the process!

But probing into the latent impetuses underpinning those achievements has opened my eyes up to the dumpster fire beneath the ostensibly glossy veneer of success. Because while almost every student these days is a "robotics champion", almost none of them have any clue *why*.

When asked why they pursue certain extracurricular activities, more than 90 percent of my applicants respond in one of three ways — because my parents told me to, because that is what other kids are doing, or because of nothing at all.

Zero self-reflection. No innate passion or desire.

The maddeningly robotic pursuit of robotics.

Increasingly, the actions that we make in our lives are determined by forces other than self. Our "highest-achieving" young people are mere marionettes, Shakespeare's proverbial poor players, strutting and fretting their hours upon the stage, many of whom burn out and are indeed heard from no more.

When I tell peers about my travels, several perceive it as a waste of time. Life should be devoted to professional progression or academic excellence, not frivolous wanderlust, they argue.

But for all of their accumulated academic wisdom, they fail to recognize one fundamental fact — that life is not a zero-sum game. I have had academic success. I am blessed to have had professional success. Life, after all, is judged by what you produce — not how you produce it.

But honestly, those things are ancillary to me.

Because you have nothing unless you have personal success. And that, to me, comes down to just three things: my individual happiness, the happiness of my loved ones, and being a good person — kind, just, charitable, and caring.

And I can promise you this. Neither academic nor professional success will ever supersede those three things.

So I conclude on this note, because — particularly as a young professional — nobody else tells you this.

If you find yourself questioning a decision, ask if it's because you question it or because others do. Ignore external forces shaping you into someone that you do not recognize. Feel free to deviate from the well-trodden path. Quit worrying.

And just optimize for what makes you happy.

Acknowledgements

This book is the sum product of many fortuitous events and experiences, for which I have many people to thank.

It started during my senior year at Duke, when I passed a flier for an upcoming TED conference on campus.

I was intrigued. After all, I had always been a fan.

A TED talk taught me to multiply two-digit squares in my head overnight — Arthur Benjamin's, "Mathemagic." A TED talk inspired me to travel abroad to Guatemala and practice MicroConsignment as an intern under the same man who delivered the talk — Greg van Kirk. A TED talk gave me confidence that it wasn't really my fault when I failed my first Math midterm at Duke, but rather the fault of the architect who designed the building such that I couldn't hear half of what my teacher was saying — Julian Treasure's "Why architects need to use their ears." Meanwhile, another TED talk helped me rebound and pass my course with flying colors with the aid of online tools — Salman Khan's "Let's use video to redefine education."

So I showed up at the audition date, vying for one of three student speaker spots at the conference.

I did not have a speech prepared.

My lack of scripting was purposeful. I always felt that rote memorization was less effective than somewhat ad-libbed delivery — the first was soulless and robotic, while the latter was from the heart. But I knew I wanted to talk about my experience on the Trans-Siberian.

And, as it turns out, the story resonated.

Two weeks later, I heard back that I was selected as a speaker at the conference, where I delivered it for posterity. The version I gave that day was slightly different than the one I had concocted at the audition. That is because, once again, I had chosen not to prepare my remarks. But, in the limited time I had, there were three fundamental ideas that I wanted to convey.

And so I did: "Lessons learned on the Trans-Siberian."

For the next couple weeks, I walked around campus and was stopped frequently by those who had watched the talk. Students and professors alike would comment on aspects of the speech that struck a chord with them, and we would discuss those topics at length. But as time wore on, the attention started to wane and life began to normalize. And that, I presumed, was that.

Several months later, I began working full-time in Seattle for Microsoft when I received an email in my inbox from a man who had watched the TED talk online and asked if I had considered turning the speech into a book. That had not been on my radar, but the idea was appealing. Ten minutes was not nearly enough time to adequately convey all I had to say about the Trans-Siberian.

I followed up with the man who subsequently encouraged me to put together a full proposal and start crowd-funding interest in the work. A few months later, I had raised several thousand dollars, attracted the interest of dozens of publishers, and inked an official deal.

The output is the book that you hold in front of you.

Perhaps it goes without saying, but I must stop to acknowledge the folks that made the journey possible.

From Gavin Ovsak at TEDxDuke, to Lee Constantine and Guy Vincent at Publishizer, to Maxim Hodak and Ksenia Papazova at Glagoslav, to all of those who pre-ordered — this would not have happened without you.

A major thanks to my parents, who supported me along the way and who held me, sometimes too tightly, to my deadlines – in particular to my mom, who made me who I am and who was the most enthusiastic reader a son could ask for.

I owe a debt of gratitude to those who invested the most financially in this effort: Kevin Kim, Abhishek Venkataramana, Marc Schwartz, and Prachish Chakravorty.

To my support system — my girlfriend Carol, who was the first to read the manuscript in its unadulterated glory, and who selflessly sacrificed many dinner dates while I stayed in to write.

To Jeremy and Avi — my co-travelers who made the trip so unforgettable and became my friends for life.

Finally, and most crucially, to you — the reader.

You've made it this far, and I sincerely hope you got something out of this book. Perhaps now you are inspired to get out and explore yourself. Maybe you agree with the lessons contained herein, and these pages resonate with you.

Or, perchance, you don't. Indeed, you may disagree with most of them. Or even all of them.

That's fine. This book isn't about convincing you of one philosophy or another. It is about making you think.

In the tech world, we like to frame problems in terms of KPIs — key performance indicators. I have many secondary KPIs — for instance, quality of writing, book sales, and laughs generated. But my North Star KPI is to get the wheels turning inside of your head.

To make you think.

To paraphrase Tupac, I don't need to change the world myself — but I do want to "spark the mind" that does.

And I hope, in whatever small way, that I was able to accomplish that.

Until next time,
Vijay

Photos

Exiting the deep subway
in Russia can be
a lengthy and terrifying
ordeal

Our first night out in Russia at the bar, Propaganda

Avi resting at Sbarro's in Moscow prior to the first leg of our journey

The otherwise unnoteworthy cannon at the Kremlin that, somewhat inexplicably, fascinated Jeremy

Avi, Jeremy, and I stand in front of St. Basil's Cathedral in Moscow in a feeble attempt to obscure its grandeur

Avi and I walking along Nevsky Prospekt in St. Petersburg en route to our hostel

On the first of two visits to the Winter Palace in St. Petersburg

Jeremy and I walking towards the Church on the Savior on Spilled Blood in St. Petersburg

Basking in the ironic solitude of the mesmerizing Lovers Bridge in Tyumen, Siberia

Slava, a fellow rider, making quick work of Avi during a game of chess on the Trans-Siberian

Taking advantage of a train stop for a quick photo, ill-attired in some baggy shorts

Jeremy and I (left) trudge slowly through the iced out Siberian city of Tyumen

Avi and Jeremy attempting to pull off the local look with some Russian hats at a shop in Tyumen

Avi and I (left) at the train station in Tyumen, waiting to embark on the next leg of the journey

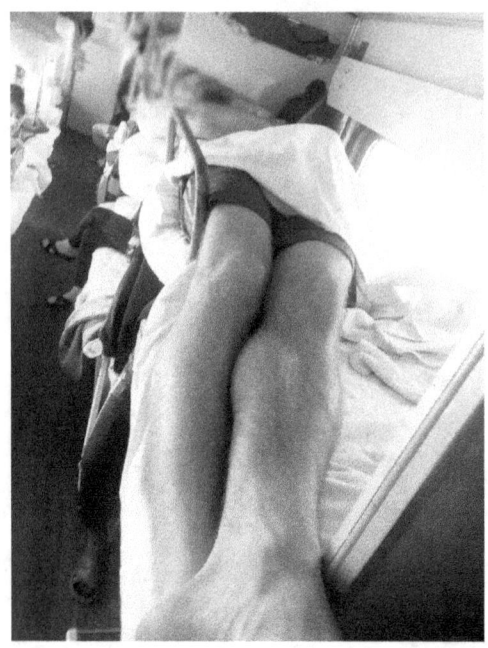

Jeremy taking a nap in his crowded train compartment, fighting against uncomfortably tight odds

Sharing the music from my iPod with a group of Russian boys headed to an ice hockey tournament east of Irkutsk

Last moments hanging out with our new companions as we approach Irkutsk

Leaving the train station in Irkutsk

Stopping for a photo at Lake Baikal

Avi (left) and I goofing off in Irkutsk before an unlikely dinner at Govinda's

Learning a Russian card game with new friends in Irkutsk

Jeremy and I lay passed out on the train, hours before crossing the border into Mongolia

Avi and Jeremy (front) walk towards our ger, a traditional tent house, on Christmas Day in Mongolia

The sun sets on a gorgeous Christmas evening in the mountains of Terelj National Park

Up close and personal with the Genghis Khan Equestrian Statue in Mongolia

CONVERSATIONS BEFORE SILENCE:

THE SELECTED POETRY OF OLES ILCHENKO

An avid reader of English-language poets such as William Carlos Williams and Stanley Kunitz, Ilchenko is one of the best Ukrainian poets writing in free verse today. His poetry is associative, flitting, and fragmentary. At times he does not form complete sentences in his poems and links words together into phrases before shifting into another thought or idea. The language of his poetry has a tendency to collapse into itself, often forcing the reader to reevaluate a word or line, to reread a previous word to focus on the poet's inner logic. This fragmentary incompleteness and permeability mimics much the way human consciousness works without the filter of the written communicative convention of sentences and grammatical structure. This "slipperiness" and rapid shifting of voice comprises one of the essential invariants in Ilchenko's poetics. The poet also flaunts many traditional poetic Ukrainian conventions. Like ee cummings he tends to avoid capital letters or punctuation such as exclamation points. One will find only commas and dashes for pauses, and an occasional period in his poems, which do not always end with the finality of that punctuation mark...

Buy it > www.glagoslav.com

Forefathers' Eve
by Adam Mickiewicz

Forefathers' Eve [*Dziady*] is a four-part dramatic work begun circa 1820 and completed in 1832 – with Part I published only after the poet's death, in 1860. The drama's title refers to *Dziady*, an ancient Slavic and Lithuanian feast commemorating the dead. This is the grand work of Polish literature, and it is one that elevates Mickiewicz to a position among the "great Europeans" such as Dante and Goethe.

With its Christian background of the Communion of the Saints, revenant spirits, and the interpenetration of the worlds of time and eternity, *Forefathers' Eve* speaks to men and women of all times and places. While it is a truly Polish work – Polish actors covet the role of Gustaw/Konrad in the same way that Anglophone actors covet that of Hamlet – it is one of the most universal works of literature written during the nineteenth century. It has been compared to Goethe's Faust – and rightfully so...

Buy it > www.glagoslav.com

Acropolis – The Wawel Plays
by Stanisław Wyspiański

Stanisław Wyspiański (1869-1907) achieved worldwide fame, both as a painter, and Poland's greatest dramatist of the first half of the twentieth century. *Acropolis: the Wawel Plays*, brings together four of Wyspiański's most important dramatic works in a new English translation by Charles S. Kraszewski. All of the plays centre on Wawel Hill: the legendary seat of royal and ecclesiastical power in the poet's native city, the ancient capital of Poland. In these plays, Wyspiański explores the foundational myths of his nation: that of the self-sacrificial Wanda, and the struggle between King Bolesław the Bold and Bishop Stanisław Szczepanowski. In the eponymous play which brings the cycle to an end, Wyspiański carefully considers the value of myth to a nation without political autonomy, soaring in thought into an apocalyptic vision of the future. Richly illustrated with the poet's artwork, *Acropolis: the Wawel Plays* also contains Wyspiański's architectural proposal for the renovation of Wawel Hill, and a detailed critical introduction by the translator. In its plaited presentation of *Bolesław the Bold* and *Skałka*, the translation offers, for the first time, the two plays in the unified, composite format that the poet intended, but was prevented from carrying out by his untimely death.

Buy it > www.glagoslav.com

Dear Reader,

Thank you for purchasing this book.

We at Glagoslav Publications are glad to welcome you, and hope that you find our books to be a source of knowledge and inspiration.

We want to show the beauty and depth of the Slavic region to everyone looking to expand their horizon and learn something new about different cultures, different people, and we believe that with this book we have managed to do just that.

Now that you've got to know us, we want to get to know you. We value communication with our readers and want to hear from you! We offer several options:

– Join our Book Club on Goodreads, Library Thing and Shelfari, and receive special offers and information about our giveaways;

– Share your opinion about our books on Amazon, Barnes & Noble, Waterstones and other bookstores;

– Join us on Facebook and Twitter for updates on our publications and news about our authors;

– Visit our site www.glagoslav.com to check out our Catalogue and subscribe to our Newsletter.

Glagoslav Publications is getting ready to release a new collection and planning some interesting surprises — stay with us to find out!

Glagoslav Publications
Email: contact@glagoslav.com

Glagoslav Publications Catalogue

- *The Time of Women* by Elena Chizhova
- *Andrei Tarkovsky: The Collector of Dreams* by Layla Alexander-Garrett
- *Andrei Tarkovsky - A Life on the Cross* by Lyudmila Boyadzhieva
- *Sin* by Zakhar Prilepin
- *Hardly Ever Otherwise* by Maria Matios
- *Khatyn* by Ales Adamovich
- *The Lost Button* by Irene Rozdobudko
- *Christened with Crosses* by Eduard Kochergin
- *The Vital Needs of the Dead* by Igor Sakhnovsky
- *The Sarabande of Sara's Band* by Larysa Denysenko
- *A Poet and Bin Laden* by Hamid Ismailov
- *Watching The Russians (Dutch Edition)* by Maria Konyukova
- *Kobzar* by Taras Shevchenko
- *The Stone Bridge* by Alexander Terekhov
- *Moryak* by Lee Mandel
- *King Stakh's Wild Hunt* by Uladzimir Karatkevich
- *The Hawks of Peace* by Dmitry Rogozin
- *Harlequin's Costume* by Leonid Yuzefovich
- *Depeche Mode* by Serhii Zhadan
- *The Grand Slam and other stories (Dutch Edition)* by Leonid Andreev
- *METRO 2033 (Dutch Edition)* by Dmitry Glukhovsky
- *METRO 2034 (Dutch Edition)* by Dmitry Glukhovsky
- *A Russian Story* by Eugenia Kononenko
- *Herstories, An Anthology of New Ukrainian Women Prose Writers*
- *The Battle of the Sexes Russian Style* by Nadezhda Ptushkina
- *A Book Without Photographs* by Sergey Shargunov
- *Down Among The Fishes* by Natalka Babina
- *disUNITY* by Anatoly Kudryavitsky
- *Sankya* by Zakhar Prilepin
- *Wolf Messing* by Tatiana Lungin
- *Good Stalin* by Victor Erofeyev

- *Solar Plexus* by Rustam Ibragimbekov
- *Don't Call me a Victim!* by Dina Yafasova
- *Poetin (Dutch Edition)* by Chris Hutchins and Alexander Korobko
- *A History of Belarus* by Lubov Bazan
- *Children's Fashion of the Russian Empire* by Alexander Vasiliev
- *Empire of Corruption - The Russian National Pastime* by Vladimir Soloviev
- *Heroes of the 90s - People and Money. The Modern History of Russian Capitalism*
- *Fifty Highlights from the Russian Literature (Dutch Edition)* by Maarten Tengbergen
- *Bajesvolk (Dutch Edition)* by Mikhail Khodorkovsky
- *Tsarina Alexandra's Diary (Dutch Edition)*
- *Myths about Russia* by Vladimir Medinskiy
- *Boris Yeltsin - The Decade that Shook the World* by Boris Minaev
- *A Man Of Change - A study of the political life of Boris Yeltsin*
- *Sberbank - The Rebirth of Russia's Financial Giant* by Evgeny Karasyuk
- *To Get Ukraine* by Oleksandr Shyshko
- *Asystole* by Oleg Pavlov
- *Gnedich* by Maria Rybakova
- *Marina Tsvetaeva - The Essential Poetry*
- *Multiple Personalities* by Tatyana Shcherbina
- *The Investigator* by Margarita Khemlin
- *The Exile* by Zinaida Tulub
- *Leo Tolstoy – Flight from paradise* by Pavel Basinsky
- *Moscow in the 1930* by Natalia Gromova
- *Laurus (Dutch edition)* by Evgenij Vodolazkin
- *Prisoner* by Anna Nemzer
- *The Crime of Chernobyl - The Nuclear Goulag* by Wladimir Tchertkoff
- *Alpine Ballad* by Vasil Bykau
- *The Complete Correspondence of Hryhory Skovoroda*
- *The Tale of Aypi* by Ak Welsapar
- *Selected Poems* by Lydia Grigorieva

- *The Fantastic Worlds of Yuri Vynnychuk*
- *The Garden of Divine Songs and Collected Poetry of Hryhory Skovoroda*
- *Adventures in the Slavic Kitchen: A Book of Essays with Recipes*
- *Seven Signs of the Lion* by Michael M. Naydan
- *Forefathers' Eve* by Adam Mickiewicz
- *One-Two* by Igor Eliseev
- *Girls, be Good* by Bojan Babić
- *Time of the Octopus* by Anatoly Kucherena
- *Soghomon Tehlirian Memories - The Assassination of Talaat*
- *The Grand Harmony* by Bohdan Ihor Antonych
- *The Selected Lyric Poetry Of Maksym Rylsky*
- *The Shining Light* by Galymkair Mutanov
- *The Frontier: 28 Contemporary Ukrainian Poets - An Anthology*
- *Acropolis - The Wawel Plays* by Stanisław Wyspiański
- *Contours of the City* by Attyla Mohylny
- *Conversations Before Silence: The Selected Poetry of Oles Ilchenko*
- *Zinnober's Poppets* by Elena Chizhova
- *The Hemingway Game* by Evgeni Grishkovets
- *The Secret History of my Sojourn in Russia* by Jaroslav Hašek
- *Mirror Sand - An Anthology of Russian Short Poems in English Translation* (A Bilingual Edition)
- *Maybe We're Leaving* by Jan Balaban
- *Death of the Snake Catcher* by Ak WelsaparRichard Govett
- *Hard Times* by Ostap Vyshnia
- *Duel* by Borys Antonenko-Davydovych
- *The Flying Dutchman* by Anatoly Kudryavitsky
- *Vladimir Lenin - How to Become a Leader* by Vladlen Loginov
- *Nikolai Gumilev's Africa*

More coming soon...

www.ingramcontent.com/pod-product-compliance
Lightning Source LLC
Chambersburg PA
CBHW071345080526
44587CB00017B/2972